C000253804

THE FACILITY OF LOCOMOTION

I

GWR 14XX Class 0-4-2T 1420.
One of the Kington 'coffee pots', now on the Buckfast Steam Railway.

THE FACILITY OF LOCOMOTION

THE KINGTON RAILWAYS

A LOCAL AND SOCIAL HISTORY

J. B. SINCLAIR & R. W. D. FENN

MID-BORDER BOOKS
in conjunction with
CADOC BOOKS
KINGTON

First Published 1991
by Mid-Border Books,
Castle Hill House, Kington, Herefordshire

ISBN 0 9518644 0 8

© J. B. Sinclair & R. W. D. Fenn, 1991

Set in 10pt Palatino and printed by
Printex, 33 Duke Street, Kington, Herefordshire.

CONTENTS

ABBREVIATIONS

FRRP	*The Further Recordings of Richard Parry the Kington Historian,* ed John Southwood, Kington, 1984
HJ	*The Hereford Journal*
HRO	The Herefordshire Record Office
HT	*The Hereford Times*
KHSP	*Kington History Society Papers*
KT	*The Kington Times*
PRO	The Public Record Office
TCS	*The Diaries of Thomas Carleton Skarratt, 1818-1909,* ed Jean Oldham, Kington, 1987
TRS	*Transactions of the Radnorshire Society*
TWNFC	*Transactions of the Woolhope Naturalists' Field Club*

'Only a few years since the picturesque woodlands, orchards, and hop-gardens, and the fertile valleys of the pleasant county of Hereford had never re-echoed the mighty heart-throbs of the iron-horse, but thanks to the energy of the leading men of the county his shrill whistle may now be heard in almost every direction, his metallic pathway having intersected the old broadlands of the Herefordshire yeomen, so as to connect almost every town and large village in the county. Railway enterprise of late has been especially directed to this part of the country, inasmuch as it is found to be the most convenient approach to the mineral wealth of Wales. Although on the borders of the Principality, till the 'Rocket' taught us how easy and cheap coal might be brought to our own doors if we would only avail ourselves of the services of those most willing labourers, like himself, we had been compelled to pay enormous prices for it, and even now in an adjoining county where they have not yet the same facilities of locomotion, those who desire to have the comfort of a good fire must pay from 25s to 30s a ton for their fuel. When steam, however, became a familiar friend, it was very soon found that the more its acquaintance was cultivated the greater was also the development of the natural resources of the county. It has not only brought us incalculable comforts but it has so improved the value of the soil that an estate or plot of land for sale in South Wales or on its borders commands the immediate notice of great capitalists, who seem exceedingly anxious to incorporate their names with it. This bespeaks well for the district, and those living in it seem to have taken the hint implied that according as railway communication increases, in reason, so will be the proportionate increase of trade and commerce and in the value of the land itself.' *Hereford Times*, March 14th 1863.

This book was written at the invitation of Mr and Mrs Peter Newman for which we would like to record our gratitude. Our thanks are also due to Mr Lawrence Banks, MA, of Ridgebourne; Mrs Jean Oldham of the Kington History Society; Mrs Gwen Gregory; Mrs Beryl Lewis; Mr Oscar Wood, MA; Dr Edward Little; Mr Thomas Fergusson; Mr Allan Lloyd; Mr Henry Pinches; Mr Keith Player; Mr Christopher Harley, MA; Lady Green Price; Mr Harry Jones; Mr Glyn Layton; Mr Bryan Lawrence, ALA; Mrs E P Jobson; Mr R Pritchard; and Mrs Cherry Leversedge for much help along the way; to the Editor of *The Railway Magazine* for permission to reproduce the map, plans, and the gradient profiles; and to Mr Norman Paton for preparing them for the press; all responsibility, however, for mistakes and omissions remains ours. We are also grateful to Mr Warwick Burton, MA, of 3 Fairway, Clifton, York YO3, for permission to use some photographs from the Mowat Collection in the Brunel University Transport Collection. Copies of these and other photographs in the Collection are available from him.

Kington, Herefordshire   November 1991

LIST OF ILLUSTRATIONS

CHAPTER ONE: CANAL & TRAMWAY [1]

K INGTON is a small country town on the Welsh Marches on the Herefordshire side of the border with the former county of Radnorshire which since 1974 has been part of Powys. Its history goes back to the coming of the Normans and its loyalties have always been as much Welsh as English so that for example its nineteenth century bank was called the Kington and Radnorshire Bank and the present day hunt is called the Radnor and West Hereford. Though it never achieved the civic status of a borough as did its nearby Radnorshire rivals of Presteign and New Radnor it prospered at their expense. Its weekly market and annual sheep sales are still important; its seventeenth century grammar school still flourishes in its comprehensive guise; its local quarries famous since the early nineteenth century for their lime and gritstone still lead in the field of technical innovation.

It has been served well both by its local gentry, like the Vaughans of Hergest Court, patrons of the medieval bards and prominent in seventeenth century Welsh politics and by incomers of initiative and enterprise like the Bankses of Ridgebourne who are still prominent in the town's life. Its tradesmen have also enhanced its prosperity and Mr AW Gamage who was once in business at 13 High Street founded the famous London firm that bore his name. National figures like James Watt have played their part, too. In the course of the nineteenth century Kington became the centre of a miniature network of railways, all of which were established by a local collaboration of gentry and tradesmen and this book attempts to chronicle the rise and fall of their achievement.

Consequently at times its pages will appear, to the reader more interested in railways themselves than in the people who planned, financed, and built them, excessively biographical. For this we seek the reader's indulgence, for as far as we know there is no other record of the local interaction of gentry and tradesmen, survivors of the charge of the Light Brigade at Balaclava, pioneers of the Eisteddfod and founders of the Cambrian Archaeological Association, the clergy, and proprietors of the local foundry, and we feel both they and their achievement deserve some account.

In 1789[2] a survey was made and a plan published 'at the expense of some gentlemen living at Leominster and Stourport' of 'an intended Canal from Kington in the County of Hereford to the River Severn near Stourport in the County of Worcester.'[3] It was to be forty-five miles long with an overall fall of 48ft, the only rise being between Leominster and Stockton Cross, 18ft and the 30ft rise associated with the Sousnat[4] tunnel, one of the three tunnels which would have to be constructed, between Leominster and Stourport. It was to start in Kington just outside the town to the north of the Leominster road and Lower Mill Farm, always travelling on the north side of the Arrow and beyond Kingsland it would cross the Lugg on an aqueduct. Its engineer was Thomas Dadford, Junior, the engineer of the Monmouth Canal.

The immediate intention, however, of the Leominster Canal Company was for its waterway to commence its journey to Stourport at Leominster but in April 1790 a meeting was held at Kington to consider extending the canal westwards in accordance with Dadford's original plan. Kington's claims won the day and it was decided to survey the country between Leominster and Kington. A combined meeting was then held in January 1791 at which it was decided to seek the necessary parliamentary legislation for a continuous canal linking Kington, Leominster, and Stourport. This was obtained in May 1791, but 'not without some opposition' and it contained a provision whereby subscriptions were to be first applied to making the canal between the Severn and Milton Cross. Then, and only then, could the residue be used for continuing the canal to Kington.

By 1796 it was apparent that insufficient funds were available and another act was obtained authorising more money to be raised. In December the canal was opened between Wharf House on the Brimfield side of Leominster and Mamble coalpit. Fourteen barges laden with coal arrived at Leominster the first day the canal was open and their cargo was sold to the inhabitants at 15/- a ton whereas before it would have cost 30/- a ton. However, there was still a shortage of funds and creditors and claimants abounded and by 1803 the company's financial reserves were exhausted. Work stopped and the company's liabilities stood at £25,000.

John Hodgkinson, who was to be the engineer for the Hay Tramway, was consulted and in May 1803 suggested the company would find it cheaper to build tramways to complete the canal's course which was still only half finished. Appropriate legislation that year authorised the construction of tramways and the raising of additional capital to reduce the anomaly of a canal running through purely agricultural country with no connection at either end.

Though some work had been done on the River Lugg aqueduct near Kingsland and in adjoining fields, nothing had been done further west, and the cost of the incomplete work between Leominster and Kington was estimated at £37,000 and that between Leominster and Stourport £83,000. A £65,000 scheme to complete the canal once again by tramroads, including one linking Leominster with Eardisley, which would have thereby become an important tramway junction, was put forward in 1834. Kington, of course, would have been by-passed, a threat which was to reappear more than once in future schemes. Happily, however, for Kington the scheme was not proceeded with. In 1860 the Leominster printer Edward J Partridge in his illustrated description of *The Route of the Shrewsbury and Hereford Railway* dismissed the canal as 'a thing of the past and has been purchased by the Shrewsbury and Hereford Railway Company for £12,000.'[5]

* * * * * *

It being obvious that the canal would not be completed Kington sought another outlet for its cast iron, agricultural produce, and good quality lime. Tramways had been proved to be cheaper than canals and the Hay Tramway from the Brecknock & Abergavenny canal at Brecon had reached Hay on 7th May 1816 and was being completed to Eardisley. Its commercial success and potential moved the principal tradesmen and leading men in Kington to come together in the Autumn of 1817 and decide to promote what was virtually an extension of this tramway from Eardisley to Kington and the lime works at Burlingjobb, three and a half miles west of the town.

The decision to seek a link with South Wales rather than the English Midlands which was the intention of the canal represents the dilemma which has faced Kington in all its aspirations for better communications, namely did Kington's economic future lie with South Wales or the Midlands? The canal and the Leominster and Kington Railway looked to the Midlands: the tramway and the Kington and Eardisley Railway to South Wales. Historically, of course, Kington being to the west of Offa's Dyke, was in *Herefordia in Wallia*, Hereford in Wales and its sympathies and loyalties have always tended to be Welsh and this is reflected, for example, in the number of High Sheriffs of Radnorshire who have come from the Kington district. It is also significant that both James Watt, Senior and Junior, men of high financial acumen if ever there were, both supported the Welsh economic orientation for Kington.

The act, which had thirty-six promoters, incorporating the Kington Railway Company, received the Royal Assent on 23rd May 1818. The authorised capital, £18,000, was divided into £100 shares and held by 34 people, all local residents. This amount exactly covered the cost of the line and remained unaltered during the company's 44 years existence. Compulsory purchase was authorised except in the case of houses built prior to 1st January that year, gardens, orchards, yards, paddocks, planted walks or avenues to a house, unless the owner agreed. Nothing was to be constructed on the Newport estate in the parish of Almeley of the Hon Andrew Foley, 1750-1818, MP, whose son, Thomas Foley was one of the company's proprietors. This last provision is understandable: Andrew Foley who had been the owner of Newport 'for a long time and has added much to its beauties by extending the walks and plantations.'[6]

There were forty-eight proprietors all of whom had a minimum of one £100 share, a considerable sum for the times. Most of them had strong local connections and all of them had ties with the counties of Radnor and Hereford. Five of them, James Davies, Thomas Foley, Sir Charles Morgan, Walter Wilkins, and the Earl of Oxford were also subscribers to the Hay Tramway and no doubt were confident of the financial advantages which would be theirs from a single tramway running from Hay to Burlingjobb. It might, however, be noted in passing that the acquisition of shares in the Company seems to have been the kiss of death: seven of the forty-eight original proprietors died in the period 1819-22. James Lloyd Harris, James Watt, Senior, Sir Samuel Romilly, the Revd Thomas Jones in 1819; Percival Lewis and James Crummer in 1821; and Thomas Foley in 1822.

The Original Proprietors of the Kington Tramway

Name & Address	Holding £	Name & Address	Holding £
Banks, Rd, Kington[7]	100	Mason, M (none given)[34]	100
Bebb, Joseph, Kington[8]	100	Mitchell, John, Kington[35]	300
Crummer James, Kington[9]	1000	Morgan, Sir Charles, Tredegar[36]	200
Cheese, EW, Ridgebourne[11]	600	Oxford, Earl of (none given)[37]	100
Cheese, John, Lyonshall[10]	500	Perry, Eliz. (none given)[39]	100
Clarke, JAG, Kinnersley[12]	200	Perry, Thos, Wolverhampton[40]	300
Coke, Rev F, Low Moor[13]	100	Price, Richd, Knighton[38]	500
Davies, James, Kington[14]	1000	Price, Robert, Foxley[41]	300
Davies, HP, Kington[15]	100	Peel, Robert (none given)[42]	200
Foley, Thos, Newport[16]	2000	Rogers, TS, Kington[43]	300
Foley, Grace Mary[17]	200	Rogers, Henry, Kington[44]	100
Fletcher, John, Stansbatch[18]	100	Rogers, Rev Jno, Bedson (?)[45]	200
Fencott, Eliz, Kington[19]	300	Romilly, Sir Saml, London[46]	500
Greenly, Mrs, Titley Court[20]	100	Sayce, Morris, Kington[47]	200

Hayward, Sarah, Kington[21]	100	Symonds, W (Jnr), Hereford[48]	200
Hutchinson, Thos, Hindwell[22]	100	Symonds, WD, Hereford[49]	200
Harris, John, Hereford[23]	300	Sherburne, John, Hereford[50]	100
Harley, Miss, Evanjobb[24]	200	Stephens, Jas, Presteign[51]	200
Harley, Miss F,Evanjobb[25]	200	Watt, James, Birmingham[52]	500
Harris, Jas Lloyd, Moor[26]	200	Watt, James (Jnr), Birmingham[53]	500
Jones, Rev Thos, Stanton[27]	100	Woolfe, Thos, Kington[54]	100
Lloyd, Thos Lewis, Kington[28]	100	Whittaker, Mrs Jno, Grove[55]	100
Lewis, Percival, Downton[29]	500	Wilkins, Walter, Maeslough[56]	300
Morris, John, Kington[30]	1500		
Meredith, John, Kington[31]	300		
Meredith, John (Jr), Kington[32]	100		
Meredith, Jas W, Kington[33]	100		

* * * * * *

The tramway followed a somewhat circuitous route from Kington to Eardisley by way of Almeley and Lyonshall, eight miles instead of five and a half miles had the route been more direct. Brilley Ridge, however, 811ft above sea level would have to be ascended by the direct route and this would have involved an average gradient of 1 in 28. The more circuitous route rose no higher than 550ft above sea level and its maximum gradient was only 1 in 59.

Progress in constructing the Hay Tramway had been greatly impeded by having several contractors and the Kington Company decided to have a single contractor who was to be responsible for maintaining the line for ten years. Three tenders were submitted and that of Hazeldine and Sayce for £14,000 was accepted. This works out at £1,750 a mile; when the Leominster Canal Company in 1834 asked John Rastrick, the engineer of the Staffordshire and Worcestershire Canal Company, to estimate the cost of completing the canal with tramways, he was asked if 'such a railway as the Brecon and Hay Railroad cannot be made at £1,200 a mile, exclusive of land.' John Hodgkinson's estimate for a twenty-four mile route for the Hay Tramway, including a tunnel, was £2,200 a mile. Thus, the Leominster Canal Company, which also needed some tunnelling, was optimistic in its hopes and the Kington Tramway Company, though it had no tunnels, did well by its contractors. Hazeldine was one of Telford's associates, but Morris Sayce, the active partner, was a Kington surveyor who 'daily superintended the men.' The services of John Hodgkinson were also used.

James Watt, Senior, as we have seen, was one of the original proprietors and the tramway went through his land at Burlingjobb, for which he was paid £33 8s. One suspects that his relations with the company, like most of his other relationships, were not always entirely smooth. In May 1818 he was sent by his agent James Crummer a copy of 'Mr Sayce's revised plan' with the modifications of the route proposed by Mr Hodgkinson as they affected Watt's land. The company would accept the revision 'provided you will give your assent to the Bill.' He was obviously satisfied and did not oppose the company's Bill and wrote on March 12th 1819, only five months before he died, aged 83, to James Davies a fellow promoter of the tramway 'My dear Sir, I am glad the railway is going on well.' He had attended company meetings and it was on his advice in October 1818 that it was decided that the ledge of the plates upon which the trams ran should be altered. These cast iron plates, each weighing 50 lbs, were three feet long and of an 'L' section. In July 1821 James Watt, Junior, who inherited his father's Radnorshire estates in 1819, asked the company to fence the tramway through his land at Burlingjobb.

The tramway was built to the same gauge as its Hay counterpart, 3ft 6ins, to allow trams to be taken through to Brecon and was opened as far as Floodgates, Kington, on 1st May 1820, though the ceremonial opening was on 18th May 1820 when, according to Richard Parry, the Kington historian, 'a band of music preceded the Tram-carriages of Coal, and on their arrival in Kington a considerable quantity was given to the poor on the Upper Cross. The company dined together at the King's Head, and the evening was spent in great harmony and conviviality.' The celebrations were somewhat premature, for the line was still incomplete and in July 1821 the company complained parts of the tramway were already out of order and that permanent bridges over the Arrow and Back Brook had not yet been erected. Consequently it was resolved that the contractors should complete the tramway within two months. And so it was, for in October 1821 the committee set up to supervise the work was 'requested to perambulate the whole line of road particularly with a view to the subject of having the blocks covered with gravel.'

There appears, however, to have been no record as to when the portion onwards to Burlingjobb was brought into use, but a meeting held on 13th May 1833 'to consider finishing and completion of the railway' suggests it was not opened until after that date. In reality the company provided its clients with a specialised highway consisting of the track; the clients paid tolls and conveyed their merchandise in their own trams drawn by their own teams of horses. In 1828 the Merediths owned 92 single and 4 double trams, valued at £576. The loaded trams were not to weigh more than 2 tons, unless the load was in one piece and trains of trams were not to travel at more than walking pace. When loaded and empty trains met, the empty one had to give way; and when both were loaded the one first reaching the passing post between the passing loops had priority. There was no travelling at night nor on Sundays, Christmas Day, Good Friday, or other days of public feast or thanksgiving. No driver was to impede the passage of the tramway for more than fifteen minutes; if he could not repair a defective tram in that time, he was to remove it from the track. The size of the trains was limited to three trams, hauled by two horses.

'On Monday, 8th March, 1841', according to Richard Parry, the Kington historian, 'a new machine made its appearance on the Tram-road:' Two men started from the town of Kington in an ingenious vehicle which they contrived to propel by means of cog-wheels set in motion by a winch, the handles of which were turned by the men who were seated in the machine. They proceeded at the rate of six miles an hour, they reached Brecon the same day, and returned to Hay about five o'Clock on Tuesday with a Ton of Coals; but leaving the machine near the Gas-house whilst they refreshed themselves, some boys began to meddle with the novel affair, and contrived to break one of the wheels, to the great disappointment of the men, who, instead of coming to Kington, which was their intention that night, only reached Eardisley, by pushing the machine before them. A scientific gentleman has stated his conviction, that a machine might be made to suit the purpose of carrying passengers and goods of every description.'[57]

No more was heard of the vehicle which seems to have been some kind of prototype of a ganger's hand trolley or velocipede.

The tramway seems to have been better managed than its Hay counterpart and the dividend it paid varied between one and 3½% and its proprietors could claim with some justification that their venture had 'developed the resources of the district and promoted the material interchange of traffic between it and the Brecon and Merthyr district.'[58] One of its merits is that coal was made more readily and more cheaply available. Coal was an obsession in Radnorshire because there was none: 'The ardency of the popular will for discovering coal in this county may be inferred from the high price it reaches in some parts of it, being fifteen times dearer than it is at the pit's mouth. The lower division (of the county) is benefited by the rail road which extends from the Brecon Canal to the town of Hay, and is continued thence to Burlingjobb in the parish of Old Radnor.'[59] Besides its domestic use, coal was also needed for the Burlingjobb lime kilns and for the gas works. According to one of the surviving tramway accounts for the six months ending 29th September 1839, 9,270 tons of coal and coke were carried from which was derived an income of £300 4s 8d. In the other direction, 1,124½ tons of lime and limestone were carried for £11 14s 8d, from which it appears the Burlingjobb lime works were able to negotiate a very competitive rate for transporting their product in what would have otherwise been empty out going trams. In September 1830 the *Hereford Journal* announced that Kington would 'shortly be lighted with that brilliant and beautiful illuminating agent, gas.' In 1851 it cost 17/6d per 1,000 cubic feet and was said to be the most expensive in the country. No wonder the citizens of Kington were beginning to want a steam railway and the cheap coal they believed would inevitably come with it.

In Kington it came to be believed that 'the Kington railway or tramway was the second greatest engineering feat in the world'[60] but when the tramway was eventually acquired by the Kington and Eardisley Railway in 1862 it was almost disused, having been unable to compete with the Leominster and Kington Railway. Its traffic with South Wales had greatly diminished without any compensating advantages coming from the north. But for the Revd James Davies 'there could scarcely be to his mind any greater proof of the power of steam that so small and fitful exertion of it as was shown in the Kington and Leominster Railway (sic) should excel and put out of the field a very respectable tramroad.'[61]

In retrospect it was argued that 'Kington throve with its Tramway; small in population, it became the centre of an important agricultural district, and it would have been hard to find any town of like dimensions which was for many years so blessed with so many advantages, owing to its public spirit.'[62] These claims were not exaggerated, for in 1808 James Davies, Edmund Cheese, and James Crummer were able to establish the Kington and Radnorshire Bank which flourished at a time when many other banks failed. The years 1825 and 1826 saw the failure of some fifty banks including one in each of Ludlow, Leominster, Shrewsbury, and Hereford, but at a well attended meeting held at the offices of the Kington and Radnorshire Bank in December 1825 it was resolved that all those who were present would do their utmost to secure for the bank 'that confidence and support to which their known opulence, responsibility, and honourable character so justly entitle them.'[63] A successful bank bears witness to a prosperous community as does the fact that a certain Richard Banks, son of Lawrence Banks, 1762-1830, of Boy's Hall near Ashford, Kent, who, having trained as a lawyer in London, almost immediately on qualifying came to Kington where he had no connections to join the practice of James Davies.

A reminiscence of 1845, by which time the town had enjoyed the benefit of the Tramway for quarter of a century, though from a different viewpoint, supports this picture: 'When a coach came to the town and changed horses, all the indolent, gaping, staring, yawning population of the town came out to look at the said horses and coach. The very horses themselves appeared to wonder what they were staring at. When the coach left the town became so quiet again the quacking of a duck or the squeaking of a pump handle could be heard from one end of the town to the other. The place, however, is since much improved and at the present time, 1845, the inhabitants are as active and lively as any town of similar size in the kingdom.'[64]

NOTES

1. Though the correct title of the Tramway is the Kington Railway, to avoid confusion with the Leominster and Kington Railway, the title Tramway has been used throughout this book.
2. This account of the Kington-Leominster Canal relies heavily on: I Cohen, ' The Leominster-Stourport Canal', TWNFC, 1957, pp. 267-285, and John Southwood, 'The Tram Road at Kington', KHSP, 1988-89, pp. 1-7.
3. HRO C 83/1.
4. Now known as Southnet.
5. Partridge, E J, *The Route of the Shrewsbury and Hereford Railway*, Leominster, 1860, p. 21.
6. *Cambrian Traveller's Guide*, 2nd ed., London, 1813.
7. The young Richard Banks, of whom much more will be heard in this narrative, had one £100 share. See chapter 2.
8. Joseph Bebb, 1759-1836, was a nail maker and carried on his business in Kington at the Upper Cross. He lived in Prospect Row.
9. James Crummer, 1749-1821, invested £1, 000 in the Tramway. Aged in 1820 seventy-one, was now at the end of his life which, despite its Irish origins, had now been closely connected with the counties of Hereford and Radnor for more than half a century. Already a JP he had just become High Sheriff for Radnorshire. Kindly and generous, so that, for example, William Ferrier, James Watt, Senior's, tenant at Stonehouse, Gladestry, reported in February 1814: 'had it not been for Mr Crummer's lending me one of his coach horses to make up a second team, I could not have got over half the work.' As a patriot at fifty he was commissioned as a Cornet in 1799 during the French Wars, having already raised three volunteer groups, and in 1804 when the threat of a French invasion seemed real enough, now a captain, he joined a cavalry corps. Since 1811 he had lived in Kington, probably at Holliday Hall in Church Street and a year later, now 62, he married his partner's sister Esther Davies, aged 28. After the foundation of the Kington and Radnorshire Bank in 1808 with James Davies, setting up the Tramway was probably the most important local venture in which he was involved and though now blind and accident prone there was little diminution in his energy. Thomas Frankland Lewis of Harpton Court in a letter of condolence to Crummer's widow spoke for many: 'We have lost a kind, worthy and valuable friend, one for whom ever since I have known him, I have had the greatest respect and regard. The fortitude and resignation with which he bore his loss of sight were truly exemplary.'

10. John Cheese, 1800-69, JP, of Lyonshall, who invested £500, was cousin to EW Cheese, another Tramway proprietor, was company secretary. His salary was £50 a year and remained so for him and his successor for the entire life of the company. He lived at Castle Weir, the house erected by his father, John Cheese, Senior.

11. Edmund Watkins Cheese of Ridgebourne invested £600. His father, Edmund Cheese, 1763-1812, was a lawyer from Lyonshall who acquired and rebuilt 1806-08 Ridgebourne in Kington. Tradition, based on the unsubstantiated evidence of Richard Parry, has it that J Milward of Hay was the architect, but the Milward brothers were more famous for tombstone inscriptions than for architecture. In 1808 he was one of the founders of the Kington and Radnorshire Bank. He was on the Tramway's management committee. The Cheeses were a prolific local family with an interest in railways. Edmund Hall Cheese, perhaps John Cheese's son, had shares in the Kington and Eardisley Railway, as did his brother Arthur Cheese, and they were both promoters of the Golden Valley railway. The Reverend John Cheese, vicar of Bosbury, near Ledbury, from 1866 until his death in 1879, was another son of John Cheese. He was to have £600 in debentures in the Kington and Eardisley Railway which ran through land he had inherited in Lyonshall parish. (See Table I)

12. John Altham Graham Clarke lived at Kinnersley Castle and is described as a farmer in an 1852 directory. He was in fact a considerable landowner who believed in railways so that in 1845 the proposed Radnorshire, Aberystwith and Welsh Midland Junction Railway was going to start on its unfulfilled route to Cardigan Bay in one direction and to Hereford in the other from The Parks in the parish of Kinnersley of which he was the owner.

13. The Revd George Coke, 1797-1863, MA, of Low Moor, now known as Lemore, Bollingham, was rector of Aylton near Ledbury, a Harley living. There is an irony in this appointment: George Coke was a descendant of Dr George Coke, who became bishop of Hereford in 1636 and retired during the Commonwealth to Eardisley where he was buried in 1646. His great opponent was Sir Robert Harley of Brampton Bryan, a staunch Puritan. The Revd George Coke's sister, Anne, married Sir William Cockburn of Downton, New Radnor, and who in the last year of his life was a director of the Leominster and Kington Railway. His son, the Revd Francis Coke, MA, a shareholder in the Kington and Eardisley Railway, inherited Low Moor and became vicar of Titley in 1877. His brother, another shareholder in this railway, Major General John Coke, CB, of the Bengal Army, lived at Low Moor in retirement.

14. James Davies, 1777-1856, was articled, as a youth of sixteen, to the Kington lawyers James Lloyd Harris, another Tramway proprietor, and Edmund Cheese in 1793 for £100. In 1804 he married Marianne, the youngest daughter by his first marriage of John Lewis of Harpton Court, and thereby he became brother in law to James Lloyd Harris. In 1806 he was made a trustee of the Radnorshire Turnpike and since this required the qualification of owning property to the value of £200 a year, though not yet thirty, he was obviously prospering. Two years later, of course, he joined James Crummer and Edmund Cheese in establishing the Kington and Radnorshire Bank. In 1809 he was appointed secretary to the newly established Radnorshire Agricultural Society comprising 'most of the principal proprietors and many of the chief occupiers of land throughout the County.' He moved to Moorcourt in the parish of Pembridge in 1818 for which his friend and client James Watt, Senior drew up plans for improving the cellars, the brewhouse, laundry, kitchens, and servants' quarters. James Watt, Junior, provided the lock to the wine cellar: 'With this you will receive the Lock for your Cellar. The Artist to

whom I confided the execution has so far outdone the usual style of Birmingham productions, that I cannot but consider it creditable to the town and as such hope you will do me the favour to accept it. If your door & walls are equally secure from invasion, I think you may without hesitation commit the precious deposit of your Wines to its custody.' The soundness of the walls was in fact the concern of Benjamin Wishlade, the Kington builder and County Surveyor for Radnorshire. The rest of his life was closely connected with Kington's railway history and is a subject of the next chapter.

15. Though 'of Kington' Hugh Powell Davies is not to be confused with his name sake, the nephew of James Davies who died aged 18 in 1818. This present Hugh Powell Davies served on the jury which at Presteign Assizes in 1805 found the unfortunate Mary Morgan of Maesllwch guilty of murdering her newborn child. She was sentenced to be hanged by Judge Hardinge.

16. The Tramway's most generous investor was Thomas Foley, 1778-1822, MP, eldest son of the Hon Andrew Foley, of Newport, Almeley. Educated at Westminster, Christ Church, Oxford, and Lincoln's Inn, he was MP for Herefordshire 1807-1818, Droitwich 1805-7 and 1819-1822. He was buried at Almeley and was remembered as 'a gentleman celebrated for his hospitality and remarkable for his benevolence of mind and affability of manners.'

17. Grace Mary Foley, born in 1775, was of course the sister of Thomas Foley of Newport, Almeley where she lived as a spinster.

18. John Fletcher, gentleman, lived at Upper House, Stansbatch, Staunton on Arrow. In 1852 his daughter, a Miss Alathea Fletcher, was farming at Stansbatch and continued to do so until her death aged 87 in 1893. Fletcher married Barbara Cheese of Castleweir Lyonshall, sister of John Cheese, Clerk to the Tramway Company, in 1802.

19. The only woman in this group each investing £300 was Elizabeth Fencott, 1765-1836, the widow of Richard Fencott of Winforton Court 'who died esteemed by all who knew him as an upright and honourable Man' and has a memorial in Kington parish church. In her widowhood Elizabeth lived in the town in Church Street.

20. Elizabeth Greenly, 1751-1843, was the widow of William Greenly, JP, of Titley Court. She endowed the National school at Titley, founded by her mother-in-law, Lady Coffin Greenly, with £1,000. A woman of considerable wealth, she left her estates and property in the counties of Hereford, Monmouth, and Breconshire to Louisa Elizabeth, Lady Hastings, wife of Admiral Sir Thomas Hastings, of whom more will be heard later, for her life time, it then went to Charles William Allen, of the Moor, Lyonshall, successfully engaged in litigation against the Tramway in 1840. He assumed the surname Greenly in 1866 and became a director of the Kington and Eardisley Railway. Nineteenth century railway history on the Welsh borders was largely a matter of family pedigrees. It was also a matter of individual houses. Thus, The Moor at Lyonshall, the home of James Lloyd Harris, one of the original Tramway proprietors, was acquired by CW Allen, a director of the Kington and Eardisley, who sold it in 1860 to Stephen Robinson, another director of the same company, who greatly enlarged it and extended its grounds.

21. Sarah Hayward may have been related to the Mr Hayward whose premises in 1833 were in Kington at Floodgates.

22. Thomas Hutchinson, 1773-1849, JP, moved from County Durham to lease Hindwell farm, Walton, Radnorshire from Thomas Frankland Lewis of Harpton Court. In 1802 his sister Mary married William Wordsworth and he was godfather to Wordsworth's second son, Thomas, born in 1806. The Wordsworths often stayed at Hindwell which Thomas farmed sufficiently successfully for him to be elected

Vice-President of the Radnorshire Agricultural Society of which his fellow Tramway proprietor, James Davies, was the secretary. His interest in securing Radnorshire better communications, not only through the tramway, but also through the provision of better roads, is reflected in his appointment to Radnorshire Turnpike Trust in 1822 on the death of his neighbour Percival Lewis of Downton House. He moved to Brinsop Court, six miles north west of Hereford, where he died in 1849.

23. John Harris came from Hereford and may have well have been a kinsman of the Kington lawyer James Lloyd Harris.

24. Miss Martha Harley of Evanjobb, one of the original thirty-six promoters of the Tramway bill, was a kinswoman of the earl of Oxford, Lord of the Manors of Evanjobb and Burlingjobb in which the Tramway terminated.

25. Miss Frances Harley, Martha's sister; they seem to have had more confidence in the Tramway's prospects than their kinsman, the Earl of Oxford, who invested only £100 in it in comparison with their £200 each.

26. James Lloyd Harris, Junior, of the Moor, Lyonshall, now known as Lynhales, was in partnership as a lawyer with Edmund Cheese, and James Davies was articled to him in 1793 at the age of sixteen. In 1797 he expressed a wish 'to relinquish his profession to James Davies on favourable terms' and in the 1798 Law List it is James Davies who is named as being in practice with Edmund Cheese in Kington. He was High Sheriff of Radnorshire in 1800, on the strength of property he had at Bryngwyn, though Jonathan Williams, op.cit., describes him as of Kington, and James Davies was his Under Sheriff. He was also related by marriage to James Davies who in 1804 married Marianne Lewis, the youngest daughter of John Lewis, JP and barrister, of Harpton Court, by his first marriage: Harris had married her elder sister. He died in 1818 and his property at Huntington was eventually inherited by Edmund Watkins Cheese of Ridgebourne. See Table II.

27. The Reverend Thomas Jones, BA, 1759-1819, was vicar of Staunton on Arrow.

28. Of Thomas Lewis Lloyd of Kington nothing is known.

29. Percival Lewis, 1757-1821, FSA, of Lincoln's Inn and Downton. His father, Edward Lewis, though MP for the Radnor boroughs from 1761-1790, was a London merchant with no local connections before acquiring the Downton estate, but had the Harley interest. He was not related to the Lewises of Harpton Court. A scholar, he helped the Revd Jonathan Williams in the compilation of his *History of Radnorshire*.

30. After Thomas Foley, next in generosity and confidence came the local businessman John Morris, 1760-1832, who invested £1,500 in the enterprise.
He is commemorated in Kington parish church as 'John Morris, late of this Town, Esq , who by his will bequeathed the noble Donation of Ten Thousand Pounds to the Hereford Infirmary and who died deeply regretted by a very extensive Circle in which he was distinguished as an able, warm, and zealous friend.' He also bequeathed £40 a year to the churchwardens of Kington who were to distribute it in bread every Sunday. His position within the town is reflected in the fact that he presided in 1830 at the public dinner given in honour of James Davies, the Kington banker and lawyer, on his retirement after thirty-two years of legal service. Five years earlier he had joined Sir Harford Bridges, bt at the public meeting held to discuss the stability of the Kington and Radnorshire Bank. They informed the meeting they had inspected the bank's accounts 'and found its balance in favour of this firm is nearly £100,000, exclusive of their private property which is known to be large,' and thereby public confidence in its affairs was confirmed.

31. The most important business man in Kington in 1819 was John Meredith, Senior,

1758-1823, who also subscribed £300. At the age of 21 he inherited the ironmongery business of his uncle Richard Meredith and a considerable fortune as well which was enhanced in 1806 when, on the death of his father, he inherited property and a successful woolstapling and cloth business. He extended the iron working on a site in Kington near the old Market Hall. He prospered and c. 1820 purchased a new site at Sunset from the earl of Oxford where he erected substantial buildings of stone to house a foundry and its workshops. He built a weir across the Back Brook and the water thereby diverted drove a water wheel which powered the foundry's machinery. The Kington Tramway contributed to the continuing prosperity of his foundry by supplying it with the coal and iron. He was also a shareholder in the Kington and Radnorshire Bank and owned property in Kington and several farms in the district.

32. John Meredith, Junior was the second son of the above John Meredith, and with his brother James was involved in building and commissioning their father's foundry. In 1828 he entered into a partnership with his brother Henry which lasted twenty years. The business flourished, Nailers' Row being built near the foundry. It was a complex of ten stone cottages and eight forges where the nailers lived and worked. He died in 1848, aged 59, and his funeral was 'attended by one of the longest processions of mourners and friends ever known in the town. The shops were all closed. Mr Meredith possessed in a high degree those qualities of heart and mind which endeared him to all who knew him'. (FRRP p.21) See Table III.

33. James Woodhouse Meredith was the third son of John Meredith, Senior. He died, unmarried, in 1826, aged 34. See Table III.

34. Of M Mason nothing is known.

35. John Mitchell, 1781-1841, MRCS. He was a Kington surgeon and married one of the daughters of John Meredith, Senior. He settled in the town in 1805 with both the recommendation and the support of the Countess of Oxford and served Kington for 35 years with ' increasing reputation and respect strictly well earned.... His hand professionally was one of the steadiest and his heart when he was called to operate was always of that temper to give as little pain to the patient as was consistent with his safety.'(FRRP p.14.)

36. Sir Charles Morgan, bt, 1760-1846, was MP for the borough of Brecon 1787-96 and for Monmouthshire 1796-1831. ' He was famed for his liberality and did much to promote agriculture in Breconshire and Monmouthshire.' He also encouraged the revival of the eisteddfod, presiding at the first 19th century eisteddfod to be held at Brecon in 1821 which was a brilliant success. He was a member, too, of the Cymreigyddion y Fenni, founded in 1833, and which, centred on Abergavenny, undertook the publication of ancient Welsh manuscripts.

37. Edward, fifth earl of Oxford and Mortimer, 1773-1848, was one of the nineteen proprietors who invested £100 each in the Tramway, the minimum investment accepted. He was the son of John Walpole Harley, bishop of Hereford, and inherited the title from his uncle. He was easily the largest landowner involved despite his rather cautious support and his main achievement seems to have been the enlargement and refacing, 'without grace of proportion or the charm of colour', of Eywood, the mansion built at Titley c. 1705 by Edward Harley, brother of the first earl. His main claim to distinction seems to have been his gift of a bowling green to the town of Presteign.

38. Richard Price, 1773-1861, MP. Educated at University College, Oxford, he was seen by Richard Parry as belonging 'to the old school of High Tories in politics'? He was MP for the Radnor boroughs for 49 years, 1797-1847, and High Sheriff in 1794. In 1808 he became colonel of the Radnorshire Volunteers and in the same year he was

at Aberedw with another Tramway proprietor, James Crummer, who claimed three shillings expenses, supervising the ballots for the county Militia which he commanded for many years. He died a bachelor and his Norton estate went to his nephew Richard Green Price who was to spend his fortune on local railways with little personal profit.

39. Elizabeth Perry is surmised to be the wife of Thomas Perry, of Wolverhampton, already mentioned as one who invested £300.

40. Thomas Perry was of Wolverhampton, though an 1852 directory names a Thomas Perry of Church Street, Kington, as a grocer and a tea and provision dealer.

41. Robert Price, 1786-1857, of Foxley, in the Herefordshire parish of Yazor, was the only son of Sir Uvedale Price, bt, 'the most brilliant of the theorists of the English Picturesque.'(Pevsner, *Buildings of Herefordshire*, p. 328.) Educated at Eton and Christ Church, Oxford, he was MP for Herefordshire 1818-41. Nothing survives of the square red brick house with its giant pilasters and arched windows of 1717 in which he lived.

42. Robert Peel appears in the Banks archives and assisted James Watt, Junior in his railway troubles. (See chapter two, p. 19, 20.) He was High Sheriff of Radnorshire in 1821 and Lord of the Manor of Grange, Cwmdeuddwr, in 1825. He lived at Cwm Elan. In 1825 he served on a committee with John Whittaker of the Grove, Presteign, (whose wife was a proprietor of the Tramway), under the chairmanship of Richard Price, MP, another proprietor, to consider plans for rebuilding the Shire Hall at Presteign.

43. Thomas Stephen Rogers was a solicitor, and in 1852 lived in Kington at Prospect Lodge in Common Close. He was clerk to the twenty-four Kington Improvement Commissioners, a body established by the Kington Improvement Act of 1829. Their main responsibilities were the paving, lighting, sanitation, and public health of the town.

44. Henry Rogers, 1757-1833, described as being ' late of the lower Swan', was presumably a Kington publican.

45. The Revd John Rogers, born in 1789, was rector of the family living of Stowe, just over the border in Shropshire and a member of the influential Rogers family of Stanage Park, near Knighton. As Lord of the Manor of Kinnerton in the parish of Old Radnor, the Tramway was for him obviously a venture of considerable commercial interest. He married into another influential family in the shires of Hereford and Radnor, his wife, Marianne, being the eldest daughter of John Bodenham, Esq., of the Grove, Presteign, which later became the home of John Whittaker.

46. Sir Samuel Romilly, 1757-1818, who invested £500, lived near Kington in Huntington Park, a red brick Georgian house with Victorian additions and now demolished. A London lawyer, he was famous for his long fights to remove the death penalty for numerous trivial offences; for state education and against the abuse of charitable funds. He was a co-founder of the *Edinburgh Review*. He acquired estates on Herefordshire and Radnorshire through his marriage to Ann Garbett, of Knill Court. However, he never lived to see the Tramway function: he committed suicide in 1818 after his wife's death and both were brought back from their London home to Herefordshire to be 'lowered side by side into a common grave at the little church of St Michael at Knill where they had been married twenty years before.'

47. Morris Sayce, 1787-1848, 'was for many years an active Gentleman in his profession and in the course of his engineering career, since he came into this County, accomplished many things which few surveyors besides himself would

have attempted. His genius in planning and forming roads and in the erection of houses (although not a practical builder) in the Italian style of Architecture, does him much credit and indicates an inherent taste for such matters. The last public benefit which Mr Sayce had in view was the removal of Turnpike Gates, in which object he was supported by many Gentlemen of eminence, and had he lived longer would have seen it accomplished.'(FRRP p.22.) He was the tramway's surveyor until 1834 and also acted professionally for both Watts, father and son.

48. Walter Symonds, Junior, was the son of WD Symonds, named below.

49. Walter D Symonds, MD, of Hereford, was High Sheriff of Radnorshire in 1793.

50. John Sherburne, 1762-1832, though 'of Hereford' was buried in the family grave at Kington. He had much property in Radnorshire and Herefordshire and had dealings with James Watt, Senior who at one time contemplated buying one of his Herefordshire estates. He was High Sheriff for Radnorshire in 1802 and the Tramway passed through his land at Burlingjobb.

51. James Stephens, a surveyor, was of Presteign, and in 1814 lived near the Shire Hall in Brick House, Broad Street.

52. James Watt, Senior, 1736-1819, the only Fellow of the Royal Society to entrust his financial affairs to the Kington and Radnorshire Bank, invested £500. His connection with Radnorshire began with his purchase of Stonehouse in Gladestry in 1798 from the Rt Hon Thomas Harley, some three years before his acquisition of Doldowlod which according to the traditional wisdom marked the beginning of his ties with the county. He had moved from Scotland to Birmingham in 1774 where he built Heathfield House in Handsworth in 1790. He became a close friend of James Crummer whilst the latter was steward and agent at Berrington Hall near Leominster, first to the Rt Hon Thomas Harley, 1730-1804, MP, the fourth son of the third earl of Oxford, and then to Anne Harley, his second daughter, who married the second Lord Rodney in 1781. Crummer acted as an agent for James Watt, Senior, first advising him on the purchase of estates in Herefordshire and Radnorshire, and then administering them for him, as well as acting as his banker. James Davies, Crummer's partner, acted as his lawyer in local matters and also enjoyed his close friendship. The interest of both father and son in local transport was not limited to the Tramway; they were also members of the Radnorshire Turnpike Trust.

53. James Watt, Junior, 1769-1848, also invested £500 in the Tramway. He was more closely connected with Doldowlod than his father and he, too, enjoyed a warm friendship with Crummer and Davies as well as with Richard Banks who joined James Davies in acting on his behalf in legal matters. The friendship with Richard Banks and James Davies flourished until Watt's death and an extensive correspondence survives between the Watts, father and son, and Crummer, Davies, and Banks. He was High Sheriff of Radnorshire in 1826.

54. Thomas Woolfe, 1762-1833, known as the 'old Banker', was a Kington maltster. Malt, along with coal, iron, lime, and timber, was one of the principal cargoes of the Tramway.

55. Mrs John Whittaker of the Grove, Presteign, is better known through her husband of whom we shall hear in the next chapter.

56. Walter Wilkins, 1741-1828, was the son of John Wilkins, the Brecon banker, and Wilkins and Co, or Brecon Old Bank, as it was known, like the Kington and Radnorshire Bank, was one of the few stable banks of South Wales and the Marches. It eventually merged with Lloyds Bank, but its notes circulated throughout the region and it was closely connected with its industrial development. Having made a fortune in India, Walter Wilkins built Maesllwch

near Glasbury, a house which was thought 'to look best at a distance.' From 1796-1828 he was MP for the county of Radnor. His son assumed the surname de Winton. He married Catherine, the third daughter of Viscount Hereford, chairman of the Hay Tramway.

57. Parry, R., *The History of Kington*, Kington, 1845, p.45.
58. HT 14.3.1863.
59. Jonathan Williams, *A General History of the County of Radnorshire*, Brecon, 1905, p.164.
60. KT 25.5.1912.
61. HT 5.4.1862.
62. Ibid.
63. RCB Oliver, 'James Davies of Moorcourt, Esquire, 1777-1856', TRS LVIII,1988, p.55.
64. Cited KT 17.9.1910.

TABLE I

The Cheese Family and the Kington Tramway

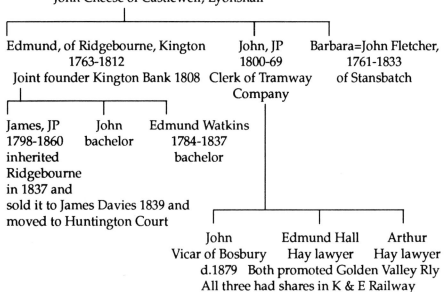

TABLE II

Tree to illustrate the interrelation of the Banks-Davies-Crummer-Harris families as Proprietors of the Tramway.

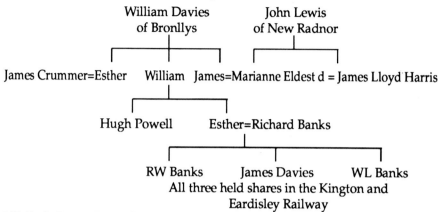

All three held shares in the Kington and
Eardisley Railway

NB Both James Watt, Senior and James Watt, Junior were customers of the Kington and Radnorshire Bank and were friends of Messrs Crummer, Davies, and Banks.

TABLE III

Subscribers to the Kington Tramway connected with the Meredith family.

John Meredith 1758-1823

Mary Ann=John		John	James Woodhouse		Winnifred=John	Henry
	Mitchell				Morgan	
1786-	1781-	1789-	1792-		1793-	1749-	1800-
1880	1841	1848	1826		1858	1824	1865

Source: John Southwood. *The Meredith Family of Presteigne and Kington 1391-1940*, Kington History Society, 1988.)

CHAPTER TWO: THE FOUNDATION OF THE LEOMINSTER &
KINGTON RAILWAY COMPANY

The earliest attempts to bring the railway to Kington and the Welsh border were the results of the initiative of the local gentry. Writing in his diary on 23rd September 1845, Sir John Benn Walsh, bt, JP, of Knill Court, near Presteign, and MP for the county of Radnor since 1840, recorded that he had ridden into Kington 'to a private meeting concocted by Jas Davies with the hope of starting a railway through Kington, Radnor, Penybont, Llangurig, to Aberystwyth. He is, I think, too sanguine about this as it appears too expensive to pay. Sayce produced a kind of sketch of the line with sections of a tunnel through Radnor Forest.... Richard Banks was to communicate with the Welsh Midland on the subject.' Ten days later the diaries continue: 'At Knill Court. At dinner Banks talked a great deal about the railway...John Whittaker called, quite alive to the prospects of the railway, as it appears that Mr Davies and Mr Banks met with great encouragement and assistance from the Welsh Midland who are much interested in promoting it.' Sir John, with considerable misgivings, was persuaded to add his name to the prospectus advocating the proposed line. He seemed surprised that the usually cautious partnership of Davies and Banks had succumbed to Railway Mania.

The Radnorshire, Aberystwith, and Welsh Midland Junction Railway was provisionally registered in 1845 with a capital of one million pounds. Great play was made in its prospectus of the slate, Baltic timber, products of the West Indies, and other imports through the developed port of Aberystwyth which would be brought back 'at very reduced prices for the inhabitants of Hereford and Worcester in return for their timber and bark.' Richard Banks and Son were named as the solicitors for the bill which envisaged the construction of the line in three parts. The main line was to commence 'at or near the Parks in the parish of Kinnersley in the County of Hereford, and terminating at or near the Town of Aberystwith, in the County of Cardigan.' Secondly, 'diverging from the Main Line at or near the Terminus of the Kington Railway, in the Parish of Old Radnor, and terminating at or near Weythell, in the Parish of Gladestry in the County of Radnor'. The intention here was to develop the Old Radnor quarries and to provide them with better facilities than those of the tramway for the distribution of their lime. Seven years before, in 1838, much useless effort was spent in boring for coal on Weythel Common. Perhaps hopes were still entertained by the promoters of this railway that coal would be found here. Thirdly, there was to be an extension, 'commencing at or near the Parks, aforesaid, and terminating at or near the Basin of the Herefordshire and

Gloucestershire Canal in the City of Hereford.'[1] Joseph Gibbs was named as the consulting engineer and M and W Sayce as the acting engineers.

It was not as fanciful as it may now seem that a main line railway should originate in the parish of Kinnersley, population 356, some twenty years before the Hereford, Hay, and Brecon Railway passed that way. In the same year, 1845, Richard Parry, the Kington historian, recorded that 'great efforts are now being made to form a new railway, to commence near the basin of the Worcester and Birmingham canal and the river Severn, in the parish of St Peter the Great, in the city of Worcester; and thence be carried by a viaduct across the Teme to Tenbury, thence to Wofferton (sic) cross, near Ludlow, and to Leominster and by the Vale of Arrow to Monkland, thence to Luntley, Broxwood, Woonton, Almeley and Eardisley.' It was then to follow the Wye through Clyro and Glasbury, and from there to make its way through Talgarth to Llanfihangel Talyllyn and Merthyr Tydfil, eighty miles of main line. Reassuringly for Kington, Parry goes on 'it is intended to have a branch from Broxwood to the town of Kington, which is a distance of 6¼ Miles. Capital required £1,500,000 in thirty thousand shares of £50 each.'[2] No more was heard of this proposed railway, though Richard Banks continued to regret its failure for many years. But had it materialised then as it passed through the parishes of Kinnersley and Eardisley en route for Merthyr Tydfil a junction with the line to Aberystwyth would have presented no problems. In December 1845 Archdeacon Richard Venables of Clyro and Llysdinam, and chairman of the Radnorshire Quarter Sessions, felt able to refer publicly to his hopes that this railway would indeed be made and would pass through the Radnor Forest.

The Jas Davies whom Sir John rode over from Knill to meet at Kington was James Davies of Moorcourt, High Sheriff of Radnorshire that year. He was a lawyer and senior partner in the much respected Kington and Radnorshire Bank of which he was a founder in 1808. He was also a former Clerk of the Peace for the County of Radnor. He was besides the friend, lawyer, and mentor in their Radnorshire affairs of both James Watt, Senior and James Watt, Junior who had extensive estates in Radnorshire. Frankland Lewis of Harpton Court near Old Radnor was Davies's brother-in-law and was at that time MP for the Radnor boroughs, both he and Archdeacon Venables had railway interests elsewhere. Richard Banks was another Kington lawyer and a partner in James Davies's practice and married his niece.[3] In 1844 he became Clerk of the Peace for Radnorshire in succession to James Davies through the intervention of Sir John Walsh. His connection with both James Watt, Senior and Junior as their lawyer had given him railway experience. In 1834 Aston Hall, the Birmingham home of

James Watt, Junior, was threatened by the proposal of the Grand Junction Railway to build a line from Birmingham to Manchester. It was. significantly perhaps, one of the first lines to be completed by Thomas Brassey who was later to build Kington's first railway, and in 1846 it became one of the five constituent companies of the LNWR. The company sought powers from Parliament to take its line through Aston Park and in his hour of need James Watt, Junior, turned to his old friends James Davies and Richard Banks. The latter went to London to supervise Watt's evidence to the Parliamentary committee: 'My time was very much occupied with the Grand Junction Railway Bill now before Parliament. The projectors of this undertaking meditated a line through Aston Park which if executed would certainly have destroyed the place. Mr Watt successfully opposed this monstrous plan and to celebrate his triumph he gave a most splendid dinner to his friends at the Clarendon Hotel in Bond St, one of the first hotels in Town.'[4]

Major John Whittaker, JP, of Newcastle Court in the parish of Llanfihangel Nantmellan, was at that time engaged in an acrimonious dispute with the dean and chapter of Worcester cathedral and Frankland Lewis over the tithes of Old Radnor, the rent paid by the Lewis family from which the the vicar's stipend was derived being 'insufficient to maintain him in that degree of rank and estimation he ought to hold in society.' He was prominent in Radnorshire affairs, being High Sheriff in 1809 and a member of the committees set up to consider plans for a new county gaol in 1819 and a new shire hall in 1825. His wife was one of the original Tramway proprietors and his brother, Abraham Whittaker, of Llanwarne, High Sheriff of Herefordshire in 1794, died without issue in 1841, and left his estates to his brother's son Henry, thereby consolidating the influence of the Newcastle Court branch of the family. Morris Sayce of Woodville, Kington, was a land agent, surveyor, and civil engineer who acted, of course, for the Tramway and for both James Watt, Senior and Junior. Nothing, however, came of the deliberations of all these people and it is significant that none of them played any part in the first successful attempt at bringing a railway to Kington.

But in July 1854 at a well attended meeting in Brecon of landowners and country gentlemen, with Viscount Hereford in the chair, there was considerable support for a proposed line which would leave the Shrewsbury and Hereford Railway at Leominster to travel again by way of Eardisley to Hay and Brecon from whence the ultimate goal would be Milford Haven. A committee was set up and at another meeting in September, a subscription list was opened, for which promises totalled

£48,000. The cost of the line, however, was estimated at £185,000 and although an application for the necessary legislation was published the scheme was abandoned in November 1854 for want of practical support.

Kington's own railway history began in earnest a year earlier, on Monday October 31st 1853, when 'a canvass was made of the town of Kington by some of its tradesmen to procure subscriptions and get shares taken for the purpose of having a Railway from Leominster to Kington, independent of any other line.' Next day a public meeting at Milner's Hotel, now the Burton, and chaired by Mr Edward Vaughan of Bridge Street, a currier and leather seller, to discuss the matter was adjourned to the next day to 'obtain the attendance of the local farmers'.

The adjourned meeting was well attended and again under the chairmanship of Edward Vaughan. A vote of thanks was unanimously passed to Lord Bateman of Shobdon Court 'for his cordial assistance and co-operation' and a six man deputation was nominated to meet him the next day at Leominster at noon. It consisted of Edward Vaughan, the currier; John Bozward, wholesale and retail tallow chandler, grocer, tea and provision dealer, and hop merchant, of Church Street; John Meek Milner, wine and spirit merchant and the proprietor of Milner's Family and Commercial Hotel at the town's Upper Cross; Francis Parker, linen and woollen draper, silk mercer and hatter, as well as an agent for the National Provident Life Assurance Company, of High Street; and two local farmers.

Lord Bateman, of course. rather than the Kington tradesmen, was the leading promoter of the railway, and the meeting which set the whole venture off had been held at Shobdon Court a week earlier on 24th October. William Bateman, the second Baron Bateman, 1826-1901, was a young man of 27 who in the year previous had become Lord Lieutenant of the county of Hereford, an office he was to hold until his death in 1901. He had recently married Agnes Burrell, 1831-1918, the twenty-two year old daughter of Sir Edward Kerrison, bt.[5]

Amongst those present at this meeting at Shobdon Court were William Robertson, engineer of the Shrewsbury and Hereford Railway, David Wylie, an engineer from Shrewsbury and who estimated it would cost £80,000 to build the line, and William Field who was in partnership with Thomas Brassey, and has been described as his 'man on the spot for the Welsh borders.' The involvement of Thomas Brassey, 1805-1870, 'the Ahasuerus of contractors', was particularly fortunate. He had already built more than 800 miles of railway, including, with Field, the Shrewsbury and Hereford which he also worked from its opening,[6] paying the proprietors for eight years 4% and half the surplus profits which so increased that in 1860 there was a 6% dividend for the ordinary shareholders. He was a sound judge in his choice of colleagues and his sub-contractors always got a fair deal. His gangers and navvies, whom he knew by name, followed him from job to job. In its obituary notice the Institution of Civil Engineers wrote of him as being 'modest and unassuming in his manners, an industrial power of the first magnitude, at once generous and exact; energetic and calm. Mr Brassey was straightforward, prompt, and honourable to the last degree.'

Lord Bateman's Leominster meeting with the Kington traders was deemed by the latter to have been very satisfactory and in the opinion of Thomas Skarratt, linen and woollen draper and silk mercer, of High Street, there were now 'good prospects of a railway being brought to our little town.' This optimism gave affairs momentum so that on November 7th, only eight days after the initial canvass, a meeting of tradesmen was held at Milner's Hotel 'to consider the best site for the Railway terminus. The third field at the bottom of Duke Street was considered the most likely to answer the purpose.'

The Kington Railway Bill passed its second reading in the House of Commons on February 20th, 1854 but the town's euphoria was abruptly dispelled ten days later: 'The little Town in a ferment through news having arrived from London that the Leominster and Kington Railway Bill would be opposed by Mr James Davies on behalf of the Tramroad Company, many were the invectives uttered against him, and a general opinion expressed of his not being worthy of the Silver plate (value £500-600) presented to him two or three years since.'[7] The supporters of the bill mobilised their forces and at a meeting at Leominster held on March 9th it was resolved that 'the opposition of Mr Davies should be met and carried out to the last'[8] and on the following day a petition praying for the passing of the bill was presented to the House of Commons. It was signed 'by nearly all the tradesmen of Kington who think the opposition is very unkind, as do also the Gentry of the neighbourhood.'[9]

Why was James Davies of Moorcourt so opposed to this particular railway? The silver plate had been presented to him in 1848 at a dinner presided over by Sir John Walsh at which 'the inhabitants of Kington and neighbourhood marked their sense of the important public benefits which he had been the means of conferring upon them, as well as their estimation of his great private worth by presenting him with a magnificent testimonial of their gratitude to him for his continued, unremitting and successful exertions to improve the district in which a long and active life had been usefully and honourably passed.'[10] Many of these exertions to improve the district had been concerned with its economic growth and the development of its communications: the Kington and Radnorshire Bank, 1808; the Kington Tramway. 1820; the Leominster Mail Coach, 1826; Kington Gasworks, 1830; the Aberystwyth Mail Coach, 1835;[11] and the construction of ten new bridges in Herefordshire and Radnorshire.

One reason for his opposition was his own long standing connection with the Tramroad Company, the main source of opposition to the bill for it understandably feared the inevitable loss of traffic and revenue to the railway. Another reason was the local belief of the gentry, which he no doubt shared, that Brassey and Field had manipulated Lord Bateman and his friends: 'After the construction of the Shrewsbury and Hereford line, which has turned out to be so profitable a speculation, the lessees saw the desirability of extending locomotive facility to Kington and accordingly made the Leominster and Kington branch.'[12] It way well have been the case, too, that if Brassey and Field had anything to do with the venture that it would not make its terminus in Kington. The 1858 edition of *Bradshaw's Directors' Guide* besides mentioning the expectation that the line would be a feeder to the Hereford and Shrewsbury railway, 'under whose auspices it had been projected', goes on to say 'it intended in the course of a year or two to continue the line to Hay and Brecon.' To do so, of course, would involve bypassing Kington. It is not surprising then that some who opposed this railway did so in the conviction that Brassey and Field, especially Field, *were* the Leominster and Kington Railway, they caring nothing about Kington, and the local directors counted for nothing.[13] Certainly they did little to win the sympathetic support of its townspeople, informing the Parliamentary committee that it was 'a little half Welsh village, barely able to grow enough agricultural produce to maintain itself, as having no trade, no commerce, nothing to export of any kind.'[14] In the eyes of the proprietors of the Tramway this cannot have been the case: 'In 1820 Kington cannot have been a contemptible village. Its inhabitants must have possessed some spirit to have devised and carried out such a work as the Kington Tramway' and that spirit was still alive in the opponents of the Leominster and Kington Railway.

Moreover, in due course, grist was added to the opposition's mill by the revelation that Brassey and Field had surveyed a line from Marston to Eardisley which would indeed have cut out Kington and that they gave formal notice of this in the autumn of 1860. James Davies's great nephew, another James Davies, of whom more will be read later in connection with the Kington and Eardisley railway, claimed that 'Mr Brassey might have no knowledge of that... but he could state it for a fact for a man's senses and memory were more keen and clear when his elm trees and his oaks were in danger.'[15]

A third factor was that the Tramway had opened up the markets of South Wales to Kington rather than those of the English Midlands and there was a belief that it was in this direction that Kington's commercial connections would be best developed. James Davies's objection to the Leominster and Kington Railway was not an objection to railways as such, but to the direction followed by this particular railway, for he was surely the anonymous 'one whom they all knew and looked up to, who had since departed from them' who had stated 'over and over again that he would subscribe £5,000 or £10,000 to a line that should connect Kington with Hereford and South Wales, as the line called the Welsh Midland would have done. The same gentleman also, on the score of its not meeting the wants of the district, and on the ground it would seriously interfere with the Tramroad determined single handed to oppose the proposed Kington and Leominster bill in Parliament.'[16] James Davies's opposition to the bill was resented by the Kington tradesmen, but it was not arbitrary and there was support for some of his arguments from within the Leominster and Kington camp itself, the manager of the railway informing the Commons committee that it was Hereford not Leominster to which Kington people wanted to go:'out of 1,100 passengers who left Kington station in a given time, 900 of them went to Hereford and the remaining 200 to the north. ' Why then, it was asked, 'in face of such a fact should they be compelled to pay 10 or 12 miles additional railway fare, to say nothing of the delay in time?'[17]

Personalities played their part, too. There is little doubt that both Richard Banks and James Davies had long memories and could recollect that it was from the earliest of Thomas Brassey's railway projects they had defended their old friend James Watt, Junior in 1834. On the other hand both men believed in the railway concept and in 1863 Richard Banks recollected that 'it was an object he had in his head for twenty years or more and one time he thought he saw a prospect of a line being made direct from Kington to Hereford. That day was for ever gone by.'[18]

The absence of Sir Frankland Lewis's support for the railway is also interesting. He was well aware of the commercial potential of a railway able to serve the limestone quarries at Burlingjobb and Old Radnor. The kilns of these quarries with those at Nash, near Presteign, consumed 2,000 tons of coal a year which until the opening of the Burlingjobb wharf on the

Tramway was brought from the Clee Hills. In 1843 he had been a commissioner of inquiry into the Rebecca riots and one of the provisions of the resulting Welsh Turnpike Act was that only half toll was to be paid on lime for farm use. He was also well aware of the inadequacies of the local roads, once recollecting that in 1848 when the Kington-Leominster road was under repair, the mud was so bad that it was said it would cost little more to have the road navigable and have a canal. The leader of a team of sixteen horses bringing stones for the road fell into the mud and it required the strength of the remaining fifteen to get him out, so unrecognisable as a horse was he that the people of Kington came to see the spectacle.[19]

Sir Frankland Lewis's disinclination to become involved in the affairs of the Leominster and Kington Railway was partly due to his healthy cynicism about 'railway sophistry' and a distrust of Brassey's financial ethics as displayed in the affairs of the Knighton Railway. 'What I have found is what a bare-faced thing it is to press people by publicly abusing them for not taking shares at the very moment when it is proposed to exonerate those who have taken shares from a liability of 20,000 shares of £20 each thus opening the door to let out persons already engaged in the concern for the purpose of letting in ignorant persons who are not so, and that for infirm pretences which are not abided by...'[20] He also had railway commitments of his own, to the Hereford, Ross, and Gloucester Railway, incorporated in 1851, and to the associated Gloucester and Dean Forest Railway whose joint link between Gloucester and Hereford was opened in June 1855. Any railway from Kington to enjoy his support would have to be with Hereford rather than Leominster.

Finally, Sir John Walsh's absence is perhaps explained by the fact that his railway loyalties eventually went to the Central Wales Railway. When funds were low and it seemed unlikely the company would be able to complete the Llancoch tunnel, between Knucklas and Penybont, he promised Richard Green Price there was £5,000 waitlng on the other side of the tunnel if they got through. They did and Sir John Walsh did invest ln the Central Wales Railway, contributing thereby to a general revival of confidence in the company which enabled it to arrive triumphantly at Llandrlndod in October 1865.

An unresolved problem was the relationship between the proposed Leominster and Kington Railway and the Kington Tramway. A meeting of the Tramway Company on March 23rd 1854 discussed the new railway and the possibility that the Tramroad shareholders would sell the whole of their interest to it. Three weeks later on April 13th Lord Bateman and James

King-King met the Board of the Tramroad Company on behalf of Leominster and Kington Railway Company 'for the purpose of buying the Tramroad Shares at a fair price so that the opposition to the Bill now in Parliament may be withdrawn. Mr Davies, Moorcourt, required £60 per share, cash down. The deputation offered £40, one half to be paid in cash, the other half in shares, which was not accepted and the affair remains still unsettled.'[21]

The Leominster and Kington Railway Bill came before the Parliamentary Committee on May 18th 1854 and Henry Meredith, the town's iron founder, and Thomas Turner, miller, maltster and seedsman, and a farmer from Downton attended the proceedings on behalf of the Bill's promoters. Richard Banks represented James Davies who left for London the next day. The following day Thomas Price, 'Agent for Bass & Co's Ales; Guinness's Dublin Porter; Clerk to the Turnpike Trustees and Kington Tramroad Company, and Banker's clerk', was summoned for the same purpose. Then on May 25th 'per Electric Telegraph and Messenger from Leominster, news arrived that the opposition had been beaten and the Bill had passed the Committee.'[22] Its passage had cost its promoters £4,654, more than three times what had been estimated, this, however, did not prevent the bells of Kington parish church being rung in triumph for two days, at the expense, it was rumoured, of the Vicar, Dr Thompson, 'another victory having been achieved over the great Mr Davies, Banks, and Co. The same manifestations of joy were manifested at Presteign.'[23]

The Leominster and Kington Railway Act allowed the construction of a single line, 13¼ miles long linking the two towns and provision was made for making a junction with the Tramway.[24] The company was empowered to raise £80,000 capital in £10 shares and to borrow, if necessary, a further £26,000. The shares were slow in being taken up, so that by 1859 only £60,000 had been subscribed of which 40 local shareholders had contributed £31,600 and five others £28,000.

The board's original chairman was Lord Bateman of Shobdon Court, a position he occupied for the first twenty-two years of the company's history. He was also involved with the Shrewsbury and Hereford Railway. Its deputy was Admiral Sir Thomas Hastings, KCB, 1790-1870, of Titley Court and 61 Upper Seymour Street, London, W. The son of a clergyman. he was born at Martley, the family living in Worcestershire. He made his career in the Royal Navy and 'by energy of mind and scientific knowledge he established a uniform system of naval gunnery' and was decorated for his services in the Crimean War. Involvement, it seems, in the Crimean War was something local railway promoters had in common. Major the Hon Charles Morgan, the first chairman of the board of directors of the Kington and Eardisley Railway, fought at Balaclava and in 1854 Thomas Brassey built a military railway at the Crimea to transport supplies and thereby saved the army besieging Sebastapol from a logistical disaster. The war over, Sir Thomas then settled at Titley Court, 'a convenient mansion and extensive park stocked with deer', and ended his days as a justice of the peace for the counties of Hereford and Brecon.

An LNWR shareholder once complained that 'in the vast majority of cases railway directors are elected for every other reason than because they have expert knowledge of railway business' and one has to admit that this was probably the case with the directorship of the Leominster and Kington Railway. As one would expect in such an area as the Welsh Marches the landed interest was well represented; so was the law, but the board had very little expert knowledge of railway business.

Two of the directors had Radnorshire connections: John Percy Severn of Penybont Hall, and Sir William Sarsfield Cockburn, bt, 1796-1858, of Downton, New Radnor. He was a generous benefactor to the parish and contributed to the restoration of its parish church in 1845. A memorial on the south wall of the sanctuary of Eardisley parish church records him as the eighth baronet of Cockburn and Ryslaw, Novia Scotia. JT Evans[25] noted that there appears to have been on record no patent or warrant of its creation and in 1905 it was listed as one of the sixty baronetcies for which 'proof is required of the due and legal creation or else proof of descent and consequent right to inherit.' An obituary spoke of him as being 'zealous in the discharge of the duties of his station, assiduous in the cause of public benevolence and of private charity, an energetic participator in the administration of the affairs of his County, and a staunch and active politician on the Conservative side.'[26]

John Percy Severn, MA, JP, DL, 1814-1900, was a lawyer and High Sheriff for Radnorshire in 1873 and illustrates the parochial nature of railway politics on the Welsh Marches by the fact that RW Banks, a principal opponent of the Leominster and Kington Railway, succeeded John Percy Severn as High Sheriff of Radnorshire in 1874. Severn inherited Penybont Hall in 1875 on the death of his father and greatly enlarged the family house which he remodelled 'in a nondescript gabled style in 1877.'

Another director was James King-King, MA, JP, DL, 1806-81, of Staunton Park, Staunton on Arrow, and MP for the county of Hereford 1852-

58.[27] In 1866 162 MPs and 53 peers were also railway directors and the Parliamentary interest of an MP on a small railway company's behalf was, of course, very desirable, the Kington railways doing well in this respect. The Leominster and Kington Railway was represented in both the Lords and the Commons by its directors. In addition it no doubt enjoyed the Parliamentary support of Henry Charles Spencer Bateman Hanbury, Lord Bateman's brother, MP for Hereford 1852-57 and Leominster 1858-62, succeeding James King-King. The Kington and Eardisley enjoyed the support, albeit briefly, of Sir Godfrey Morgan, MP for Brecon, and Sir Richard Green Price, MP for Radnor. Other directors were: Elias Chadwick, JP, of Pudlestone Court, near Leominster; John Samuel Bannister of Weston Court, Pembridge; James Bedford, the manager of the National and Provincial Bank, of Broad Street, Leominster; and Thomas Bristow Stallard, also of Leominster where in Broad Street he carried on the business he had set up in 1837 as an importer and wholesale wine merchant.

The only member of the board of directors connected with Kington was Henry Meredith, 1800-1865, of the Foundry. He and his brother John ran the family business as a partnership until the latter's death in 1848. A man of many parts, he is described in an 1852 directory as 'linen and woollen draper, silk mercer and hatter, ironmonger, iron founder, tin plate worker, nail manufacturer, agricultural implement manufacturer and wheelright.' In August 1862 his gunpowder store in Duke Street, near the Oxford Arms, exploded, breaking many windows and damaging several roofs in the town, but no one was hurt, for which cause there were services of thanksgiving in both the parish church and the Methodist chapel.

The company secretary, at the not inconsiderable salary of £497 pa, was William Daggs, manager of the Leominster branch of Worcester City and County Banking Company, Limited, and an agent for the Phoenix Fire and Scottish Life Insurance companies. He later became the secretary of the Leominster and Bromyard Railway and a JP and was to be described by an inquiry of 1877 as 'a very able and earnest officer.' The company's offices were in Corn Square, Leominster.

On November 1st 1854, exactly a year after the original meeting to canvass opinion about the railway, a shareholders' meeting was held at Kington 'to consider the best means to carry out the day's festivities at the cutting of the first sod which operation is to be performed by Lady Bateman.' The meeting came to few conclusions and was, in typical Kington style, adjourned, but when it met again a few days later at the Oxford Arms it was still unable 'to come to a decision on certain matters' and there was another adjournment. What happened at that meeting is unknown but the matter was taken over by the directors of the railway company who held a meeting on November 20th 'to consider the best means of causing the cutting of the first sod to pass off with eclat when it was decided a general holiday should be given, a procession form at the Oxford Arms, walk to the field, re-form, then proceed to Milner's Hotel where a Champagne Luncheon will be prepared, and all partaking thereof to pay 5/-. In the evening a Ball at the Oxford Arms under the patronage of the Lady Langdale and James King-King, Esq.'[28] The directors were also considering more important matters and on 14th November they accepted Brassey and Field's tender to construct the whole line for £70,000 and to work it from its opening to 30th June 1862, paying the shareholders 4% per annum.

The first sod was cut on November 30th. 'The morning being fine brought crowds of country people to Town. About 1 o'clock the Procession formed, headed by the children of the National and Sunday Schools. After them, various flags; parading four navvies carrying the wheelbarrow on a platform, the King's Head Club, the Oddfellows Club, the Tradesmen of Kington, and lastly the carriage of the aristocracy taking part in the ceremony. A little after 1 o'clock all assembled on the Ground and the ceremony was performed by the Lady Bateman in a workmanlike manner.[29] Unfortunately a shower of rain came on just at the time and marred the pleasure of not a few. At Milner's Hotel a splendid Champagne Luncheon was provided.... and at night a large Ball at the Oxford Arms. The town itself was decorated with evergreens and several excellent arches spanned the entire streets. For the school children tea was provided and the inmates of the Union had a jolly blow-out of roast Beef and Plum Pudding.'[30] The directors of the railway contributed £87 14s 8d to these 'Kington Festivities.'

NOTES

1. HRO AL88/21,22-3.
2. See Table A.
3. Banks Archives.
4. Parry, op.cit., p.45.
5. See Table B
6. For goods in July 1852 and passengers in December 1853.
7. TCS p.9.
8. Ibid p.9.
9. Ibid pp.9,10.
10. HT 16.12.1848
11. 'At a Meeting of the Inhabitants of the Town of Kington assembled this fourth day of October 1834 at the House of Mr James Pugh in the said Town, John Meredith,

Esquire, in the Chair, Resolved: That the thanks of this Meeting be gratefully tendered to James Davies Esquire for his exertions in time past in having procured for the Inhabitants of the Town of Kington a daily post. Resolved: That it is the anxious wish of this Meeting that the Kington and Worcester Mail Coach be continued from hence to Aberystwith and that Mr Davies be earnestly requested to use his influence in obtaining the consent of the Postmaster General. Resolved: That if the consent of the Postmaster General should be obtained this Meeting pledges themselves that they will aid and assist in every possible way the continuance of the Mail from Kington to Aberystwith.' There follows the signatures of eighty-nine local citizens. Banks Archive.

12. HT 14.3.1863.
13. HT 5.4.1862.
14. Ibid.
15. Ibid.
16. HT 14.3.1863.
17. HT 5.4.1862.
18. HT 14.3.1863.
19. Cited by Howse, WH, *Kington Herefordshire*, 1989, p.11.
20. Banks Archive.
21. TCS p.12.
22. Ibid, p.14.
23. Ibid, p.14.
24. Clinker, CR,'The Railways of West Herefordshire', TWNFC XXXV, 1957, p.288.
25. Evans, J.T., *The Church Plate of Radnorshire,* Stowin the Wold, 1910, p.78.
26. Quoted by Richard Parry, FRRP p.53, but he does not name his source.
27. Born at Weybridge, Surrey, 1806, he was the eldest son of the Revd James Simkinson, who assumed the name of King in 1837. Educated at Balliol College, Oxford, he became Deputy Lieutenant of the county of Hereford in 1845.
28. TCS pp.23,24.
29. With a silver spade, costing £12 which, with the wheelbarrow, is now in Leominster museum. She was to use her skills again in August 1858 when she cut the first sod of the Knighton Railway for which ceremony the spade wheelbarrow are now in Llandrindod Museum.
30. Ibid, p.25.

TABLE A

The Banks Dynasty

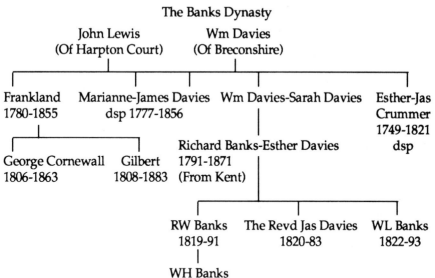

TABLE B

The Bateman Family and the Lord Lieutenancy of Herefordshire

Lord Viscount Bateman=Anne,   d.Charles E of Sunderland & grand d of
1727-1774   John, Duke of Marlborough

John, Lord Viscount Bateman=Elizabeth,   d. Sir Jeremiah Sambroke, bt
1721-1801   1724-1802
baron of Culmore in the
kingdom of Ireland, Privy
Counsellor, 'many years
Lord Lieutenant of
Herefordshire',

William Bateman Hanbury=Elizabeth, d. Ld Spenser Stanley
1780-1845   1791-1882   Chichester 2nd son of
                                                                          1st Marquess of
1st Ld Bateman of   Donegal & of Lady Harriett
Shobdon Court   d. of 7th Earl of Galloway
Kelmarsh Hall,
Northants,'Many years
Lord Lieutenant of
Herefordshire'

William Bateman=Agnes Burrell, d. Sir Edward
1826-1901   1831-1918   Kerrison, bt
Second Lord
Bateman of
Shobdon, Lord
Lieutenant of
Herefordshire 1852-1901

CHAPTER THREE :
BUILDING THE LEOMINSTER & KINGTON RAILWAY

P rogress in actually building the railway between Kington and Leominster was rather less enthusiastic than the preliminary celebrations. The contract with Brassey and Field was not sealed until May 1855. It was difficult to acquire the land upon which the railway was to be built: partly because of the tightly knit nature of local society the company was reluctant to use its legal powers of acquisition and partly because, with a confident eye on the future, it had been decided to purchase enough land for double track, though at present a single line was deemed sufficient. Moreover, the Crimean War made money more expensive. Thus, eighteen months after the inaugural celebrations only eight and a half miles of single track had been laid, linking Leominster with Pembridge and only a portion of this was in use, for carrying coal. Permission for this had been given to Field as partner in charge of the work in October 1855.

The shareholders were informed that further funds were needed to complete the work, though David Wylie, the line's engineer, reported that it could be at Kington by November if 'the company were put in immediate possession of all the necessary land.'[1] The problem, in Lord Bateman's view, as the company chairman, was that Radnorshire was not making an appropriate financial investment to the venture. Radnorshire, he argued, would be the main beneficiary of the line getting to Kington, but it was from Radnorshire that support 'which they had so fondly anticipated' for the project was least forthcoming. 'This', he said, 'was partly due to the influence of an opposing scheme, the Central Wales Railway, which, pretending to show that greater advantages would be derived from it than from their own line, was warmly taken up by parties of unquestionable respectability and with unlimited funds at their command. Not-withstanding all these promises and prospects, at the eleventh hour the scheme hit the ground. They therefore hoped that, such being the case, they might count upon the support of these gentlemen from whom they were led to hope so much at the commencement of the undertaking. If Radnorshire did not pay its way, then the line had little prospect of getting to Kington.'[2] It was not surprising that the rumour had got about that now the line had arrived at Pembridge, there was no intention to take it further. To allay this suspicion it was decided that the existing line would not be opened for passenger traffic until it did in fact reach Kington.[3]

Another reason given for the lack of financial support for the company was the rumour that Field and Brassey would finish the line, if needs be, themselves as a private investment so there was no need for the public to risk investment. Consequently Field informed the meeting: 'I beg distinctively to say we shall not take any more shares and that we shall not ourselves finish the line. According to our agreement we are not bound to pay you 4% dividend until the line is opened.'[4]

A tenant farmer from Old Radnor confirmed the lack of support for the railway from his neighbours and Mr John Percy Severn of Penybont Hall, now the board's only Radnorshire director, undertook to canvass the county for more support. Because of the company's parlous financial position the directors were taking no fees, even so it had, unfortunately, 'been found that the accounts were not so altogether satisfactory as the Directors were led to anticipate. There was a great complication of books, and much that the Directors thought that it would be better to have put into a more tangible shape, collected and properly scheduled.'[5] Consequently auditors had been appointed to examine thoroughly the company's accounts.

By April 1856 the company's funds were almost exhausted and Brassey and Field had to rescue it by advancing £10,000 at 5% interest to continue the line to Kington. They already held £20,000, one quarter of the whole capital, and it is not surprising that Brassey later complained that he had lost heavily on his arrangements with the Leominster and Kington Railway. The weak financial position of the company meant that when the directors of the Tramway approached it in December 1856 with an offer to sell their line, the Leominster and Kington had to decline the offer for they were 'not in a position to entertain so desirable a proposition.'

Locomotives were first used on the line in January 1856 and on Saturday, 13th June 1857 'Mr Field, the contractor, brought the first fifty tons of coal along the Railway for sale at Sunsett Station amidst the acclamations of the people.'[6] The occasion, as far as Kington was concerned, was something of a non-event because the trucks were steam hauled only as far as Titley, from thence it was literally a matter of horse power. It was the intention that the line should open in May, 'but due to the weather and other circumstances' it was not until July 11th that 'the first steamers reached Kington Station, in the presence of many hundreds',[7] laden with timber, stone, and other materials for completing the still unfinished station buildings. The line was inspected on July 22nd by Colonel Yolland for the Board of Trade which would not authorise its opening for public traffic because a level crossing had been made at Pembridge instead of the bridge provided for in the Act. By dint of compromise, hectic correspondence, and further inspection the opening of the line was agreed to, providing the company obtained a second act legalising the crossing.[8] Thus, on Monday 27th July 'the Road was opened for passengers, or rather, for the Directors and their Friends and the Public free of cost. At 2 o'clock the train reached Sunsett Station with 32 carriages and 2 engines of great power, bringing with them 1,500 persons from Leominster and other stations.'[9] The train was due to have left Leominster on the arrival at 12 05 pm of the express from Shrewsbury, in which case it took almost two hours for the 13¾ mile journey.

Tradition has it that Brassey worked the Leominster and Kington with two locomotives, *Bateman* and *Brassey*. Perhaps these were the two locomotives 'of immense power' mentioned by Thomas Skarratt in his account of the opening of the railway. Those who travelled in this train paid one shilling and sixpence for the privilege and amongst those so to do was the Revd JN Walsh, MA, headmaster of Lady Hawkins' School and lecturer at the parish church and who preserved his ticket for posterity. As a clergyman he had an appropriately sustained faith in the facility of locomotion which survived another fifteen years until 1871 when he bought £50 shares in the Kington and Eardisley Railway.

It is recorded that 'there were present nearly 15,000 persons who received the train with loud huzzahs and much cheering. The Shrewsbury Band came along, 36 persons with flags and banners. Carriages from Hay, Builth, Rhaeadr, Knighton, Presteign, and Cardiganshire brought numbers early in the morning. The Luncheon took place at the Oxford Arms, Admiral Thos. Hastings in the Chair, Lord Bateman and his brother Captain Hanbury[10], late MP for the County of Hereford, was among the Company; they left at 4 o'clock to dine together at Leominster.'[11] Five pounds was collected in the town to pay for a band to parade the streets and the bell ringers. Some fifty pounds was collected for the parish poor, for dinners for the inmates of the Workhouse and for the pupils of the local schools, and for entertainments for the townsfolk, Mr Milner as the town's leading hotelier hired a band from Presteign for his assembly room which 'was filled to suffocation.'

The train left Kington at 4 o'clock for the return journey to Leominster where Lord Bateman presided over Dinner at the Royal Oak Hotel at five and for which tickets were available, 'including a bottle of wine and dessert' at 10/-. A train back to Kington left Leominster at 9 pm. The celebrations at Kington continued next day with 'rustic sports... such as wheelbarrow racing, running for crowns, going up poles for mutton, etc. Captain Tilfet, the County Chief Constable, lent a strong body of police to assist to keep the peace.'

The railway opened for regular passenger and goods service on August

20th when the first train from Leominster reached Kington at 7 30 am.
Captain Galton, a Gentleman of great talent and experience,[12] had officially
inspected the track four days previously and had 'pronounced the Line to
be 'all right'[13], but the stations at Kington and Titley were still incomplete.
There were also stations at Titley, with a crossing loop; Marston Halt;
Pembridge, with a crossing loop; Ox House, a private station for the
Bateman family of Shobdon Court; and Kingsland. The immediate effect on
the Tramway was to increase its traffic beyond Kington so that a new 'Hinds
Patent Framed Weighing Machine' had to be ordered for use at Kington in
1857. A toll keeper's cottage was built in 1858 and an additional passing
place was provided at Stanner.

The receipts averaged £120 a month for the first six months of the line's
history, but in September 1859 Brassey complained that he was losing £1,500
a year on his working contract and he offered to pay £2,000 to be released
from it. The contract had three more years to run and the company was not
prepared to suspend it. But the possibility of other arrangements had to be
explored. An offer of amalgamation with the Shrewsbury and Hereford
Railway was declined and the West Midland leased the line from July 1862,
guaranteeing, like Brassey, a 4% dividend and a share of the profits. In 1863
the West Midland, itself a combination of three smaller units, dating from
1860, amalgamated with the Great Western which revised the terms of the
agreement with the Leominster and Kington in August 1865, taking 60% of
the gross receipts. The times were not financially propitious and the Great
Western, as it often did, could strike a hard bargain and within twelve
months on Black Friday, 11th May 1866, the bankers Overend, Gurney, &
Company who had financed numerous railway contractors, failed to open
for business with known debts of £10m. Peto & Betts stopped the same day
with debts of £4m. In the opinion of the *Economist* 'the plain truth of the fact
is that Overend, Gurney, Unlimited for the sake of high interest, took bad
securities, and in consequence someone must reap the consequence of that
badness.' One of those who did so was Thomas Brassey who lost £1m in the
crisis, though he still died one of the richest men in the country in 1870. A
document of 1861[14] suggests that by then Kington station had acquired the
appearance of busy country railhead. The station building itself was
substantial and included a commodious stationmaster's house. The
Tramway was still functioning and mention is made of its sidings, a carriage
dock, wharf, water tank and premises as well as offices and cranes. There is
also mention of turntables and platforms. The joint owners of the site are
given as the Leominster and Kington Railway Company, lessees Thomas
Brassey and William Field, and the Kington Railway Company. Brassey and
Field, the South Wales Coal Company, and the Hereford Coal Company are

named as the occupiers of the site. In 1869 Mr George Parmee, 1842-1918, became its stationmaster and goods manager at the remarkably young age of 27. Born in Hereford, he joined the Leominster and Kington Railway in 1861 at Kington, moving to Pembridge in 1863 as stationmaster, aged 21. He then remained at Kington from 1869 until his retirement in 1908, returning for a brief period during the Great War.

By 1869 it was accepted that the future of the railway, despite what was claimed at the shareholders' meeting that year to be a steady increase of traffic, though it only produced the decidedly modest revenue that financial year of £899, lay in extending the line 'to bring it into connection with the Welsh and other railways.' Contrary to the accepted wisdom of the day the goal of this expansion was not Milford Haven. In Lord Bateman's opinion 'the anticipation of Milford Haven becoming, in the time of the present generation, the great sea port for this part of the country, was the most unmitigated delusion that ever was in the world. And for this reason: the Great Western Railway, without which nothing could be done in that direction, had adopted Swansea as their port. Any allusion he had ever made at the Great Western Board to Milford Haven had been pooh-poohed. The Manchester[15] or other people might talk about Milford Haven, but the Great Western having adopted Swansea as their port, nothing would ever go from that port to Milford Haven except a branch line.'[16]

A line to Presteign was the ambition of both the Leominster and Kington Railway and the Kington and Eardisley. Until that was achieved the Leominster and Kington Railway assured the public its line 'ran within a few miles of Presteign the county town of Radnorshire.'[17] At the same time Richard Banks informed the supporters of the Kington and Eardisley Railway that 'from a junction on that line it was contemplated to extend the railway communication throughout the county of Radnor.'[18]

When it became apparent that for financial reasons the Kington and Eardisley Railway could not implement its intention of building the line for which powers had been obtained by its Act 1864, the authority of which was extended to July 1870 by another Act in 1868, the Leominster and Kington obtained an Act in July 1871, authorising the construction of such a line from near their Titley station to a place near the county gaol at Presteign, 5 miles 22 chains away. The site is now occupied by John Beddoes school. The first sod was cut at Presteign on Thursday January 4th 1872 by Miss Edith Green Price, deputising for her mother Lady Green Price who was indisposed. Luncheon followed in the Market Hall with the Honourable Arthur Walsh, MP, in the chair. The streets of the town were decorated and bread and meat distributed to the poor. The estimated cost of the Presteign branch was £40,000 on which the Great Western guaranteed payment of the interest as part of an agreement of July 1871 to work the line for 60% of the gross receipts. The Leominster and Kington company was empowered to raise capital of £40,000 in shares and to borrow £13,000.

At the same time, attempts were also made to strengthen the Leominster and Kington board, the most important acquisition being the Revd Sir Gilbert Frankland Lewis of Harpton Court, a residentiary canon of Worcester and absentee incumbent of Gladestry, Moccas, and Monnington. He had joined the board, and that of the Kington and Eardisley, by 1872. Canon Gilbert Frankland Lewis was Chaplain to James Davies, the great opponent of the Leominster and Kington Railway, when the latter became High Sheriff of Radnorshire in 1845. His father, Sir Frankland Lewis, had been conspicuous by his absence from the company's affairs. The acquisition of Gilbert Frankland Lewis together with that of RW Banks by 1888 marked the growing unity of the Kington railway interest. RW Banks's son, William Hartland Banks, also eventually became a director.[19] His son, Mr Richard Banks, recollects his father's golden director's key entitling him to free first class travel on the line. Another sign of this growing unity of purpose was the membership of Stephen Robinson of Lyonshall, chairman of the Kington and Eardisley Railway Company.

Meanwhile it was decided that the Presteign terminal on the gaol site would be inconvenient and with the consent of the Board of Trade and local interests it was moved half a mile into the centre of the town to its position in what became known as Station Road. The errors of New Radnor where the station waited for its passengers in splendid isolation 'without the city walls' was not repeated at Presteign. The contract for building the line was let to Perry & Company of Bow, London, builders of St Thomas's Hospital and the Royal Academy. Charles Chambers was the main contractor.

The services of three hundred navvies were enlisted and construction involved 'wonderfully steep' gradients up to 1 in 43 and, though only five and three quarter miles long, twenty bridges and as many cuttings, culverts, and embankments. Dynamite was used to blast the long and very deep cutting at Roddhurst and at Wegnall the line had to be lifted on a long embankment over the flood plain of the Hindwell and Back Brooks. At Titley Junction complex sidings and cross overs were needed as well as a sixty frame signal box. However, all these works and the collapse of the Forge Crossing bridge over the River Arrow, a two arch stone structure carrying a huge earthen embankment, in early 1874, caused further delay.

When rebuilt, the brick-lined arches of the bridge were 150ft long, 25ft wide, and 12ft high to their crown. They carried a 75ft deep ash infill. All this resulted in the need to raise a further £5,000 to prevent the contractor from immediately withdrawing, even so, the railway line was completed within the four years allowed by its Act.

The *Hereford Journal* was much taken by what it deemed to be the scenic beauty of the line: 'the combination of vale and wood-clad hill, with delicious peeps of shady green retreats among the trees which in many places skirt the line again is one that does not often greet the traveller's eye from a railway carriage window.'

The inspection by Colonel Hutchinson however did not take place until 2nd September 1875 and his only comment was that the bridges appeared to have been made unnecessarily strong which was ironic in the light of the collapse of the bridge at Forge Crossing. Some feel he might also have mentioned the solidity of Presteign station, built in 'the metropolitan style' in Nash and Bath stone. It had a heavy roof awning and monumental chimney stacks. The final cost of the line was £50,750, more than £10,000 over budget. Later, Dansey Green Price, speaking at the unveiling of the memorial obelisk erected to the memory of his father on Hawthorn Hill, between Norton and Knighton, in December 1889, was to claim that 'very few people knew what a share Presteign had of having no railway at all, but his father and himself found the £5,000, the bridge (at Forge Crossing) was cleared, and the country above saved from being flooded, and the Presteign Railway was accomplished.'[20] Tradition has it that one workman was killed in the disaster and James King-King, MP and vice chairman of the company, was an eye witness. His extensive Staunton Park estate was close by and he said that as the valley was exceedingly narrow and there was only room to clear one half of the debris at a time, 'they must finish one half of the bridge before they could remove the debris of the other half.'

On August 28th 1875 the *Hereford Times* was able to assure its readers that the opening of the Presteign branch, after various delays, was definitely fixed for the 9th September and to inform them that 'the day will be kept with public rejoicing and observed as a general holiday in the town. The poor will be entertained, three clubs walk in procession, a luncheon prepared in the middle of the day at which the High Sheriff of the county will preside. The county and borough members are both invited to attend.'

The opening did indeed take place on September 9th and the county press carried full, though differing, accounts of the occasion which indirectly record the social condition of much of the local population, in need of beef, bread and coal, as they do the events of the day:

'At half past nine a procession was formed.The regimental band in uniform took the lead, followed by a large wagon containing a fine ox, decorated with laurel berries, hops, and the usual appropriate festooning. Next was a wagon containing a dressed sheep, then another with bread, and several carts with coals, together with a large and expectant crowd brought up the rear. After this quaint procession had marched round the town the contents of the wagons were distributed to the poor by ticket.

Precisely at 11 45 a large procession was formed at the Shire Hall for the purpose of meeting the special train which brought the various distinguished visitors. The procession was, of course, the demonstration of the day. It was formed of the members of the New Club, the Odd Fellows, the Foresters, the junior members of each of these societies, the committee for carrying out the day's arrangements, visitors, tradesmen, inhabitants of the town, and schoolchildren. The New Club, Odd Fellows, and Foresters, of course, paraded their distinguishing, costly, and appropriate banners.'

The Sunday Schools represented were St Andrew's church, Wesleyan, Primitive Methodists, and the Baptists, who were marshalled and kept in excellent order by their teachers. Meanwhile a number of Ladies and Gentlemen had gone down from Presteign to Titley, the end of the branch, in a saloon carriage, to meet the Hon Arthur Walsh, MP and pick up the Marquis of Hartington. They left by a special train, gaily decorated with flowers, at 11 15. Mr Walsh left Eardisley by a special train and was met at Titley by the Marquis of Hartington, Sir Richard and Lady Green Price, General Sladen, the High Sheriff....

The train proceeded through Kington under the charge of Mr Grover, the Superintendent of the line to New Radnor, in order to fetch Sir Gilbert Lewis, whose indisposition, however, unfortunately prevented his attendance.'

Back in Presteign the train discharged its collection of passengers which formed itself into yet another procession which made its way to 'a spacious tent' behind the Castle Hotel for 'a sumptuous luncheon'. A dinner was also provided for the navvies and others employed on the line in another tent on ground adjoining the Radnorshire Arms. There were, of course, the inevitable speeches and from that of the Hon Arthur Walsh it was apparent that the line was not yet quite complete: 'a very small link now remained to be completed to make the line the shortest route from the centre of the iron trade and the coal fields of South Wales' and it was his hope that 'it would be many years before they had to celebrate the completion of the branch of our great railway system which would not be inferior to any in England.' The missing link was at Titley Junction where it was impossible without shunting to travel direct from Presteign to Eardisley. Apparently despite the strenuous Parliamentary efforts of both Arthur Walsh and Sir Richard Green Price before the appropriate Parliamentary committee, the Kington and Eardisley Railway had been denied running powers over the Leominster and Kington's metals to Presteign. This was due, no doubt, to opposition, not from the two local companies, but from larger interests beyond Kington and Presteign, and Arthur Walsh expressed his hope that 'in time friendly relations would exist between the different companies and that they might derive the full benefit from it.' Dansey Green Price, in his speech, noted that in all it had taken more than twelve years to bring the railway to Presteign and had involved the acquisition of four Acts of Parliament and the employment of three different engineers. Ironically, perhaps Sir Richard Green Price in proposing the health of the chairman and directors of the Great Western Railway 'referred in complimentary terms to the assistance the company had rendered in this undertaking.'[21] It was not to be long before the alleged duplicity of the Great Western Railway was to be blamed for the failure of the Kington railways. The celebrations of the day concluded with sports and 'a capital exhibition' of fireworks.

Like the building at Presteign all the station buildings of the Leominster and Kington Railway were far more substantial than those of the Kington and Eardisley, and included stationmasters' houses at Kington, Titley Junction, Pembridge, and Kingsland. With the exceptions of Kington and Presteign which were entirely stone built, they were built of brick with facings in dressed stone. The stationmasters' houses at Kington, and Titley Junction were an integral part of the station building. They each had a kitchen-living room, and a scullery, bathroom, and coal house on the ground floor and two bedrooms and a box room above. At Kingsland and Pembridge the stationmasters' houses, though offering similar accommodation, were detached buildings in alignment along the platform with the station building.

The station at Titley Junction had a separate ladies' waiting room, with its own lavatory, as well as a general waiting room and booking office. There was also a detached corrugated iron parcels office. A small canopy projected over the platform from the station building and the opposite platform had no shelter. The Old Radnor Trading Company had a siding and an office. There was also a weighbridge, with its own brick and wood office, for the use of carts and drays. There was no mains water supply, and water was delivered daily in milk churns until 1947 when a 13½ ton six wheel glass lined water tanker was installed. The overall passenger and goods traffic accommodation was similar at Kingsland and Pembridge, though Kingsland had a goods shed, a lamp room, and cattle pens. The goods shed at Pembridge is a particularly handsome brick building with decorative Gothic arches, each surmounted with a dressed keystone. The level crossings along the line had keepers' cottages alongside them. Where they have survived, as at Waterloo Mill near Kingsland, despite enlargement and alteration, they can still be usually detected from their substantial central brick and stone chimney stacks. The crossing cottage at Marston was demolished in 1991 after being earlier badly damaged by fire.

None of the station buildings at Almeley, Stanner, Dolyhir, and New Radnor included accommodation for a stationmaster, and were all simple, somewhat austere, stone built, rather lofty, single storey buildings, divided into a waiting room, with a fire place, and a booking office, warmed by a stove. Access to the building was by a large central double door, which at Stanner was on the platform side of the building. The arrangement at Lyonshall, because the railway line ran there on an embankment, was rather more complicated. The station was two storied, with a ground floor entrance hall and stairs to the platform and waiting room. Its slate-covered roof was hipped and there was a large round-headed upstairs window at each end of the building, looking up and down the track. Simple as they were, these buildings were at least more substantial than the station at Moreton on Lugg on the Shrewsbury and Hereford line which was apparently originally accommodated in a hollow tree trunk.

From the beginning Sir Richard Green Price saw one of the Presteign line's roles to be a feeder to the other local lines. Others, however, had more grandiose aspirations, at the expense of the New Radnor Railway, for the new line, and an anonymous correspondent to the *Hereford Times* wrote:

'It certainly strikes me that more must be made of the line and that it is destined to form part of the direct through route to Aberystwyth and the Welsh coast. To a superficial observer the following would appear to be the easiest and simplest mode of carrying out this very desirable scheme. The GWR company to make a line from Presteign to Dolau on the Central Wales line, run over the Central Wales line to Llandrindod, to construct a new line from Llandrindod to the Mid Wales line near Doldowlod, to run over the Mid Wales line to near Rhaeadr, then to construct a new line to Strata Florida on the Manchester and Milford Railway and run over that railway to Aberystwyth. This will provide an almost direct communication without constructing any great amount of new line and would increase the traffic on certain of the Welsh railways which would no doubt be glad for any accession to their earnings. By taking advantage of the valleys the proposed new lines could probably be constructed without any insurmountable difficulties to encounter.'[22]

There was nothing particularly innovative in this argument. It had been anticipated by the Radnorshire Railways Bill of 1865 which generated the *Memorial* to the Kington and Eardisley directors in November 1864.[23] The financial results of the first days of working were deemed to be very satisfactory: £70 was taken in the first eight days of working although 200 tons of coal had already been brought over the line by the contractor. But the receipts of the line for 1876, its first complete year of operation, only amounted to £1516 14s 1d, or £5 8s 0d per mile, per week. The company was in a state of financial crisis for the affairs of the main Leominster to Kington line were little better.

Thus, in 1877 the company commissioned Price Waterhouse and Company to investigate its financial position. The Leominster and Kington Railway had entered an arrangement in 1865 with the GWR to work the line on the assumption that gross receipts of the line would be of a guaranteed minimum £8,500 a year. But, according to the GWR this was only once achieved, in 1873, when the gross receipts amounted to £8,513 3s 10d, or £12 5s 0d per mile, per week for the thirteen mile line.[24]

The receipts from 1867-1876 were:

1867...£6,984	2s	4d
1868...£7,434	1s	4d
1869...£7,656	1s	5d
1870...£7,291	17s	6d
1871...£7,426	2s	2d
1872...£7,827	18s	0d
1873...£8,515	3s	10d
1874...£8,065	10s	6d
1875...£7,921	2s	1d
1876...£8,386	4s	10d

They were deemed 'a disappointing result even after allowing for the possible diversion of traffic via Eardisley when regard is had to the fact that at least two Lines which should be feeders exist beyond, ie: the Presteign Branch and the Kington and Eardisley Railway to New Radnor.' The GWR now required the extension of the platform and sidings at Titley, additional sidings at Pembridge, and a water supply at Kingsland, involving the Leominster and Kington Railway in an expenditure of upwards of £1,300. 'If they have a right to demand these works, there is of course no limit to the possible demands of the future, and seeing that the Company have exhausted their capital powers for the Main Line it becomes a very grave question on which it would be better at once to obtain counsel's opinion.'

The opening of the branches to Eardisley, New Radnor, and Presteign necessitated a new station at Kington which was no longer a terminus. This was built slightly to the north of the original terminus, part of which still stands having served as a goods depot before becoming part of the new industrial estate. Built by the Kington and Eardisley Railway, the new station was jointly owned with the Leominster and Kington. It was much smaller than its predecessor which continued to house the stationmaster. Built sideways-on to the main platform, it was a single story structure, with small canopies to the front and rear. There was now a dispute over apportioning the cost of its buildings. It had two platforms and a passing loop. A signal box and a small engine shed were also built, the latter being some hundred yards to the west of the new station. Bridge works were also involved for which the Kington and Eardisley Company claimed £393 as well as half the cost of 'the double line, platforms, sheds, etc' at Kington. The total cost of these works was £965 and so in all the Kington and Eardisley's claim was for £875 10s 0d. The Leominster and Kington's Company secretary, William Daggs, however, stated to Mr JA Mann, who was carrying out the investigation for Messrs Price Waterhouse, 'he has no knowledge of any debt due to the Kington and Eardisley Railway Company', to which Mr Mann added his own observation that 'it is apparent that the Messrs Green Price or their advisers made arrangements without the knowledge of the Leominster and Kington Board or officers.' Mr Mann advised compromise: 'Litigation should be avoided if possible and I suggest that Mr Clarke be authorised to meet Mr GW Owen and endeavour to agree on fair terms of settlement.'

In 1889 Dansey Green Price claimed that every penny for building the Presteign branch had come from the Green Prices, father and son, but Mr Mann in his examination of the Company's affairs thought 'the position of the accounts between the Messrs Green Price and the Company in regard to the Presteign Branch is peculiar.... These gentlemen intended and did in fact take upon themselves the responsibilities of the construction of the Branch and of all the financial operations connected with it and that the Directors consented to go on with the extension only on the understanding that the Company should not suffer in any way from it. Such an arrangement is extremely difficult to enforce in the absence of contracts or written agreements.' At this time, of course, Dansey Green Price was the company solicitor, a post from he resigned on the outbreak of the dispute. A solicitor like his father, he had never joined the family firm. He was admitted in 1861 and became a partner in the London firm of Crawley, Arnold, and Green of Whitehall which acted at times for both the Leominster and Kington Railway and the Kington and Eardisley. From 1872-1876 he practised alone in Presteign, then in 1876, at his own request, his name was removed from the solicitors' roll. It was restored in 1882, but according to the records he never practised again and one wonders whether there is any connection between these decisions and this dispute.

The matter now in dispute between the Green Prices and the Leominster and Kington Railway was whether or not their liabilities had been discharged with the completion of the line. The Green Prices maintained they had no further liability and Mr Mann warned 'it is extremely improbable that the Company will succeed in fixing them with such a liability without a very distinct and written contract.' This however did not exist.

The Green Prices had taken out £21,000 in shares in the company and were now in a court action seeking £7,671 9s 6d for money they had lent it to pay the land owners over whose land the railway ran £5,700, and £1,191 9s 6d owing in interest to debenture holders and the bank. The Company, however, maintained that 'the alleged deposit of £5,700 was never made with the Company though a Loan was taken by the Messrs Green Price of the Worcester City and County Bank who credited the proceeds to an account opened in the name of the Messrs Green Price, the Company having no sort of control over the account.'

Mr Mann's conclusion was that the Green Prices' demand for £7,671 9s 6d was excessive: the transaction with the Worcester City and County Bank was a personal one on their account. Moreover, the amount actually received from the Green Prices to pay landowners was £4,887 14s 6d and not £5,700, and the Green Prices admitted themselves that they were to provide the interest on the debentures up to the date of the completion of the branch. This meant they had wrongly included £419 18s 5d in their account. Mr Mann's recommendation was that they should be paid £4,887 14s 6d in shares, with interest from 9th September 1875, the date when the line was completed. 'I cannot help thinking that the Messrs Green Price have acted hastily in commencing proceedings. Their having previously rendered two accounts to the Company, the first showing £10,128 10s 11d and the second £9,009 18s 5d as due to them while the statement of claim shows only £7,671 9s 6d to be due, and the necessity for amending the statement of claim, all confirm this view. I trust therefore that when the facts are placed fairly before them those Gentlemen may be induced to accept the terms indicated by me.'

Were the Green Prices to accept Mr Mann's recommendations then he felt 'there is nothing in the Company's financial position to excite alarm, though it is evident that the Company's capital is insufficient for it to provide for its engagements and that therefore the financial arrangements of the Company need the closest scrutiny. Of course if Messrs Green Price intend regardless of the consequences to the Company to press their claim and Mr RD Green Price intends to render a large Bill of Costs the position will be altered and some remedial measures will be necessary......It appears to me, looking at the matter from the outside so to speak, that it should be mutually advantageous to the Company and the Messrs Green Price to effect an amicable settlement, but even this will necessitate real or supposed concessions on both sides.'

Laura Meredith, Richard Green Price's fifth surviving daughter, with an uncharacteristic lapse of charity, wrote in her diary about her half-brother Dansey's woeful extravagance and speculations in railways and other things.'[25] Over the railways it was like father, like son. Besides his connections with the Knighton Railway, the Central Wales Railway, and the Central Wales Extension Railway, Richard Green Price was at one time chairman of the Kington and Eardisley Railway, and on the boards not only of the Leominster and Kington, but also the Worcester, Bromyard, and Leominster; the Aberdare and Central Wales Junction Railway; and the Lugg Valley Railway. At the time of the dispute he and his son Dansey were also closely associated with the Golden Valley Railway which was just being built. Dansey was also a director of the Kington and Eardisley; the Worcester and Aberystwyth Junction Railway; and chairman of the Shropshire Railways. He said of the railways: 'By all means open your arms to them. There is no law against polygamy in railways.' He took up £50,000 in share capital and debentures in the Golden Valley Railway and few, if any, of these lines prospered. Richard Green Price's personal estate when he died in 1887 was £11,258 6s 4d, modest enough when one remembers the fortune he once possessed in an estate of 8,774 acres with an estimated rental in 1873 of £7,688 a year. When Dansey died in 1909 he left, in addition to the settled estate, property of gross value of £444, and net personality of £30. His son had to spend 'sixty years repairing all the damage... a mortgage of some tens of thousands on the family estates was finally paid off in 1960'[26] Thus the question arises whether in 1877 the Green Prices could afford to drop their case against the Leominster and Kington Railway.

The first occupants of the new engine shed at Kington were two class 517 0-4-2 tank engines which were to work the line for the best part of the next sixty years. No 202 was not withdrawn from service until 1928. Their Kington predecessors were two Crewe type 0-6-0 tank engines, built by Jones and Son of Liverpool. They had 5ft 6ins driving wheels and 14ins and 20ins diameter cylinders. Both locomotives were transferred to Swindon in 1874 and 229 went to Westbourne Park and 230 to Oxford, but their GWR careers were short-lived and they were both withdrawn from service on 1878. In running the railway the train staff, one engine in steam principle was followed, with the later addition of a block telegraph between Kington and Leominster(Kington Junction). Staff and token working were introduced in 1882 and electric staff between Titley and Kington in 1903, electric working being extended to Leominster (Kington Junction), in 1911.

The railway, for all its failing fortunes, was a matter of local pride, and Thomas Skarratt, the Kington draper, for example, recorded in his diary for 11th February, 1880 how he 'planted fifteen shrubs, the gift of Mr Bodenham, at Sunset, on the embankment of the Railway Bridge, the side next the town', in an early and public spirited example of landscape gardening. Benjamin Bodenham, a solicitor who lived in Kington at North Place, Church Street, was a man of many parts, for besides being a director of the Leominster and Kington Railway, he was also clerk to the Board of Guardians; assistant clerk to the County Court; Steward of the Manor of Eardisley; and agent to the Imperial Fire and Crown Life Assurance Companies.

The Leominster and Kington Railway Company continued until July 1898 when it was amalgamated with the Great Western Railway. The eighty-ninth and final half-yearly meeting of the company was held on Monday, August 29th at the company's offices at Leominster, Stephen Robinson being in the chair. It was resolved 'that the following Dividends for the half year ending 30th June 1898, be declared: Four per cent on the Ordinary Shares, Four and a half per cent on the Preference Shares, and Four and a half per cent on the Presteign Branch Shares, and that the same be payable on the 1st

September as usual. That the Amalgamation of this Company with the Great
Western Railway having been sanctioned by Parliament as taking effect from
the 1st July last, the surplus funds remaining in the hands of the Company,
after payment of any claims against the Company, be divided as a further
dividend on the Ordinary Shares, on the 1st January next.'

NOTES

1. HJ 20.2.1856
2. Ibid.
3. Ibid.
4. Ibid.
5. Ibid.
6. FRRP p.41.
7. Ibid.p.41.
8. This was obtained in April 1859.
9. FRRP p.41.
10. Henry Charles Spencer Bateman Hanbury, educated at Eton and Brasenose
    College, Oxford, where he was Fellow of All Souls 1848-62. He had a commission
    in the Lifeguards from which he retired as a captain in 1859. He was ADC to the
    Lord Lieutenant of Ireland in 1858 and became Deputy Lieutenant of the county
    of Hereford in 1860.
11. FRRP p.41.
12. FRRP p.42 gives, incorrectly, the inspector's name as Captain Peckhill.
13. Ibid. p.42.
14. HRO Plans of the Kington and Eardisley Railway Company deposited with the
    Quarter Sessions, 1861.
15. ie The Manchester and Milford Railway Company.
16. HJ 20.2.1856.
17. *Bradshaw's Directors' Directory*, 1859.
18. HT 14.3.1863.
19. In 1897.
20. HT 4.12.1889.
21. Clinker, op.cit., p.292, alleges that not a single fact in any of the speeches was
    accurate. The justice of these remarks is disputable and inaccurate reporting a
    more likely source and a comparison between the accounts given in the *Hereford
    Times* and the *Hereford Journal* is worth while. The present authors have relied on
    the account of the *Hereford Journal* rather than that of its rival, the *Hereford Times*.
    The Marquis of Hartington had been a local MP and had £300 of shares in the
    Kington and Eardisley Railway. We have also made much use of the work of
    Beryl Lewis, 'The Railway Branch Line from Titley Junction to Presteign, a short
    history', *Kington History Society Papers*, 1981-82, pp. 8, 9.
22. HT 18.9.1875.
23. See Chapter 5, p 62, 63.
24. PRO RAIL 363/6.
25. 'The Recollections of Laura Meredith', ed RWD Fenn and NT Roberts, TRS LV
    1985, pp 68ff.
26. Mowat, CL, *The Golden Valley Railway*, Cardiff, 1964, p.84 and n. 12,

CHAPTER FOUR: THE KINGTON & EARDISLEY RAILWAY

O n May 3rd 1851, two years before the inauguration of the Leominster and Kington Railway Company, Isambard Kingdom Brunel wrote to the Revd James Davies, né Banks, of Moorcourt, who had sought his advice on building a railway from Kington to Eardisley:

Dear Sir,

I think the project you suggest demands consideration but the seasons for railway planting and reaping have become as fixed as those of any crops and this is the time of repose when it is unwise and indeed impolitic to sow anything. About August when the fate of this year's projects begins to be ascertainable will be time to consider what may be desirable.

Yours very sincerely,

IK Brunel[1]

What was politic and desirable became apparent, at least for James Davies and his colleagues, with the opening of the Leominster and Kington Railway for goods and passenger traffic in 1857 and the passing of the Act in 1859 authorising the construction of the Hereford, Hay, and Brecon Railway signalled the inevitable demise of the Kington Tramway. The proprietors of the Kington Tramway and others argued that what was now needed was a standard gauge railway from Kington to Eardisley where it would join the new railway between Hereford and Brecon and maintain the town's long established commercial relations with South Wales from whence a line now linked Merthyr Tydfil and Brecon. There was also a need for a direct link with Hereford itself, the county town. 'The Leominster and Kington Railway was all very well in its way, and no one would attempt to deny that such a railway connection with Kington was better than none. But there were long heads and sagacious minds then in existence who saw from long experience that the Leominster line was not Kington's proper direction, that its traffic was naturally with the south rather than the north, that its tendency was to Hereford, its county town, and to Hay, Brecon, and Merthyr '[2]

As a preliminary in September 1861 WL Banks, James Davies's brother, offered to purchase all the shares of the Tramway Company at £40 cash for every £100 share or £60 worth of shares in a new company dedicated to converting the Tramroad where practical into a railway using steam locomotives from Kington to Eardisley, with a branch into the Leominster and Kington Railway near The Sheriffs, a farm near Upper Marston. The Tramroad from Kington to Burlingjobb, however, was to remain narrow gauge and horse-drawn. As an alternative, an offer was made to the Tramway Company of £6,000 cash or £9,000 worth of shares in the new railway company. This scheme came to nothing and in December 1861 the Tramway Company resolved that the Tramway should be sold to Thomas Savin, the railway speculator, and that the eleven remaining proprietors should each receive £45 for every £100 share they owned. This was to be paid on 30th September 1862, after the passing of an Act to promote the Kington and Eardisley Railway. Their clerk was also guaranteed £50 a year for life. In March 1862 at a special meeting of the Tramway Company it was resolved to petition the House of Commons in favour of the Bill necessary for winding up its affairs and in the following month it also petitioned the House of Lords. It was also resolved that the seal of the company should be affixed in July to a list of its shareholders and forwarded to the new Kington and Eardisley Railway Company.

On Wednesday, April 2nd 1862 a public meeting was held of the inhabitants of Kington and neighbourhood at the town's Oxford Arms Hotel 'for the purpose of promoting the scheme for the construction of a railway from Kington to Eardisley, joining the Hereford, Hay, and Brecon line and a branch from Lyonshall to Marston on the Kington line. There was a very large attendance.' It included the local gentry and clergy[3], lawyers[4], the Post Master[5], the bank manager[6], the clerk to the Kington Tramway Company.[7] There were also some Kington tradesmen and farmers present.[8] The strongest family interest was, inevitably, that of the Bankses; The Revd James Davies, Richard Banks, RW Banks, and, of course, WL Banks. The principal outsiders were James Williams, MD, FRCS, of Brecon, who was to become a director of the company, and Thomas Savin, who was already active in the area as the contractor for the Hereford, Hay & Brecon Railway. No one seems to have come to represent the interest of Eardisley.

The two moving spirits behind the project were the Revd James Davies who was elected chairman of the meeting, though he protested that 'in the boat he did not care whether it was No 1 or No 8 and would do anything in his power to bring the boat safely into port', and his brother William Lawrence Banks, who could not be thanked enough 'for acting so truly for the place of his birth.'

The Revd James Davies, JP, MA, 1820-1883, the second son of Richard and Esther Banks, was educated at Repton and Lincoln College, Oxford.

Ordained by the bishop of Gloucester in 1845 be became, after a period as perpetual curate of Christ Church in the Forest of Dean, Master of Ludlow School in 1852,. He remained at Ludlow until he inherited Moorcourt in 1857 from his great-uncle James Davies, of whom so much has been written in the previous chapter, together with all his lands in the parishes of Pembridge, Lyonshall, and Almeley. A condition of his inheritance was that he took the surname Davies. At Moorcourt, we are told, 'he zealously fulfilled the duties public and private of a landowner.' He was by nature, though, more a scholar than a proprietor of a substantial estate. Like his two brothers, he contributed to *Archaeologia Cambrensis*, the journal of the Cambrian Archaeological Association in which he was prominent for many years and a member of its committee. He also contributed to the *Quarterly, Saturday*, and *Contemporary Reviews*. He was a generous churchman and in 1860 built at his own expense an elaborate tin tabernacle for the use of those who lived on his Moorcourt estate, officiating in it regularly until incapacitated by a paralytic seizure in 1883. He became a prebendary of Hereford cathedral in 1875.

William Lawrence Banks, 1822-1893, was the third son of Richard and Esther Banks and so was James Davies's younger brother. Educated at Shrewsbury school in 'its palmiest days', he developed into something of a versatile and eccentric genius. As an artist his talents are nowadays less appreciated than once they were, but his 'Eight Sketches in the Vicinity of Kington' lithographed and published by Charles Humphreys, the Kington publisher and stationer in 1846, are a useful pictorial record for the local historian, including, for example, a picture of Moorcourt, the home of his brother James. Drastically remodelled in the 1860s, the house no longer exists.

He became a solicitor, practising in Brecon where he was mayor in 1859 and 1861. In 1856 when his brother James inherited Moorcourt, he inherited Bronllys castle, Talgarth and land in Breconshire from their great-uncle James Davies. There is an irony in this, for WL Banks had already conceived the ambition of becoming a patron of the railway, rather in the same way as others became patrons of the arts, and he inherited much of the wealth he used in fulfilling this ambition from James Davies who had so opposed the building of the Leominster and Kington Railway. 1863, however, for all the potential of the Kington and Eardisley Railway, was a sad year for him, seeing the death of his wife, Mary Jane Williams of Ystrad Meurig, whom he had married in 1850. His belief in railways is indisputable: besides having directorships in the Hereford, Hay, and Brecon and the Kington and Eardisley Railways, by 1875 he was also on, or had been on, the boards of the Afon Valley, the Anglesey Central, the Brecon and Llandovery Junction, the Brecon and Merthyr Tydfil Junction, the Dulais Valley, the Mid Wales Railway, the Shrewsbury and Hereford, the Knighton Railway, the Central Wales Railway, the Corris Railway, the Midland Counties Railway, the Denbigh, Ruthin, and Corwen Railway, the Neath and Brecon, the Newport and Usk, the South Essex, the Whitby, Redcar, and Middlesborough Union Railway, and the Swansea Vale, Neath, and Brecon Junction Railways.

In later life, his long white beard, Scotch cap, knickerbockers, and stockings made him a distinctive figure at archaeological and artistic gatherings. A good raconteur with a sense of humour, he is remembered for often quoting the verse which embodied his philosophy of life:

> Believe not each aspersing word
> As some weak people do,
> But always think that story false
> That ought not to be true.'

Besides James Davies and WL Banks, the other four original directors of the Kington and Eardisley Railway were: The Hon Major Godfrey Charles Morgan, MP, of Tredegar Park, Newport, and the Company's first Chairman; GS Herbert, Esq, of Westgrove, Blackheath, Kent; RK Penson, Esq, FRIBA, of Dinham House, Ludlow; and JJ Williams, Esq, MD, FRCS, of the Mount, Brecon. Two at least of these directors are of particular interest.

The Hon Major Godfrey Charles Morgan, 1831-1913, served with distinction in the Crimean War, 1854-56, and as a captain in the 17th Lancers took part in the famous cavalry charge at Balaclava. He was MP for Brecon from 1858 to 1875 when he succeeded to his father's title as the second Lord Tredegar. He was created Viscount Tredegar in 1905 and died unmarried. We have already met his grandfather, Sir Charles Morgan, bt, as one of the original subscribers to the Hay Tramway and one of the first proprietors of the Kington Tramway, with a holding of £200.

Richard Kyrke Penson, 1816-1886, was a member of the dynasty of architects founded by Thomas Penson, Senior.[9] His father, Thomas Penson, Junior, was the architect of the original 1848 Shrewsbury station, remodelled in 1903-04, on the Shrewsbury and Hereford Railway, and as county surveyor of the counties of Montgomery and Denbigh was famous as a bridge builder. His father's churches were rather less acclaimed, that of Llanymeynech, for example, being described as 'a wondrously crazy demonstration of the Neo-Norman fashion.'[10] Thomas Penson, Junior, had two sons, Richard Kyrke Penson and Thomas Mainwearing. Richard succeeded his father as county surveyor for Montgomery and was active in Chester, Oswestry, and West Wales.[11] In 1886 he certified the application of the Radnorshire architect SW Williams for election to the Fellowship of the Royal Institution of British Architects. He held several other railway directorships, including the Bishop's Castle Railway, the Buckley Railway, the Hoylake Railway, and the Wrexham and Connah's Quay Railway. His younger brother, Thomas Mainwearing Penson, 1818-1864, specialised in domestic and ecclesiastical architecture and was active in the nineteenth century revival of half-timbered architecture.

The Brecon surgeon John James Williams was also a director of the Sidmouth and Budleigh Salterton Railway, and it is perhaps significant that at the same time WL Banks was chairman of the Sidmouth Railway. JJ Williams was also a member of the Cambrian Archaeological Association which grew from *Archaeologia Cambrensis*, first published in 1846 and it is remarkable how many of those connected with the early history of the Kington and Eardisley Railway were also prominent members of the Association. The three brothers RW Banks, WL Banks, and the Revd James Davies all held office and were regular contributors to the journal, RK Penson was the Association's local secretary for the Marches, SW Williams contributed several articles and undertook some important archaeological investigations, and GC Morgan and JJ Williams were both members. There was in fact an overall tone of scholarship amongst those connected with local railways: Percival Lewis of Downton, Edmund Cheese, James Davies, and James Lloyd Harris all subscribed in 1805 to Theophilus Jones's *History of the County of Brecknock*, Sir Samuel Romilly was one the founders of the *Edinburgh Review,* and Sir Charles Morgan was a patron of the Eisteddfod.

On the other hand, George Sowerby Herbert, of Gloucester Terrace, West Grove, Blackheath, London, SE seems to have had no pretensions to scholarship. He appears to have been involved with the Kington and Eardisley Railway purely as a financial speculation. He was listed in the 1861 Census returns as a 'Stockbroker and member of the Stock Exchange', and invested £200 in ordinary shares.

Henry Meredith, the Kington iron founder, and John Bannister, of Weston, near Pembridge, were both reported as being ready to become directors of the new company, notwithstanding their position as directors of its rival, the Leominster and Kington. But in the event they appear to have withdrawn from their agreement, though they both bought shares. On the other hand, several of the principal shareholders in the Tramway had announced their willingness to take them in shares in the Kington and Eardisley, amongst whom were Lady Langdale, James Cheese of Huntington Court, The Revd F Coke of Lemore, Bollingham, and RW Banks. James Davies invested £1,000, WL Banks £2,000, and Arthur Cheese, £700. The Kington currier, Edward Vaughan, who worked so hard to further the cause locally of the Leominster and Kington Railway, bought £900 worth of shares.

The proposed new railway was not without its opponents, especially amongst the shareholders of the Leominster and Kington Railway. To minimise their opposition, having arrived at Lyonshall from Eardisley, it was from thence to follow the direction of the Tramroad into Kington to the Tramway's wharf at Sunset. This means it was to have a separate terminus from the Leominster and Kington Railway even though this would have involved knocking down the Nailers' Cottages built by the Merediths for their employees near the site of the new station. There was also to be a branch from Lyonshall through the Castle Weir, the Whittern, and the Sheriffs[12] to Marston where it would join the Leominster and Kington Railway and it was this part of the Company's plans which so aroused the Leominster and Kington's opposition. 'Any one', at least in the opinion of James Davies, 'would have thought that the advantages of such junction, the food which the branch would minister to the Kington and Leominster line, would have made that company thankfully accept it.'[13] Davies claimed that several of the Leominster and Kington Railway shareholders had given plain proof that they shared this view and that others had not hesitated to say so when talking on the subject. All the same, the Leominster and Kington Railway opposed the Kington and Eardisley Railway Bill in both houses and and attempted to get the clause struck out which had been inserted to allow traffic over their line by way of a junction at Marston. The opposition, apart from 'a small shabby petition from some landowners, the chief name on it being that of Mr Percy Severn[14], who was the owner of from two to four acres of land in the parish of Lyonshall', did not come so much from local landowners as from Thomas Brassey and William Field who had leased the Leominster and Kington Railway and who feared 'ruinous competition.'[15]

However, the Bill, opposed 'so feebly, so childishly, so frivolously that one could not help wondering what tactics could have dictated such a course',[16] received the Royal Assent in June 1862, incorporating a new company with a capital of £100,000 in shares and £33,000 by borrowing, and empowered to acquire the property of the Kington Tramway.

The contractor was Thomas Savin, 'the contractor of the Hereford, Hay, and Brecon Railway, also of several Welsh railways, who, we understand, has at present more than one heavy continental contract on hand. Doubtless the work could not possibly have been placed in better hands, for Mr Savin has greatly distinguished himself in several very important undertakings, and he has happily the means at his command to proceed without delay. With so energetic a board of directors and so eminent a contractor, the line will unquestionably be soon completed, probably in the course of a twelve-month.'[17]

It is said that Savin, a draper by trade and self-taught contractor, 'financed railways on promises', embarking upon ambitious schemes without caution or judgement and carrying boards of directors with him and borrowing money recklessly. But he had charisma and the directors of the Kington and Eardisley Railway were captivated by it, being both deaf and blind to warning signs. In 1863, at the very time of the inauguration of the works on the Kington and Eardisley, Savin was in trouble with the ill-fated Bishop's Castle Railway which he started in 1861. He was paid £14,000 in ordinary shares and £500 in cash to defray Parliamentary and engineering expenses. In March 1862 he received a further £5,000, but made no physical progress with the line whatsoever and the whole enterprise has been described as 'a marvellous imposture.'

There is little doubt that Thomas Savin's connection with the Kington and Eardisley Railway was for some an impediment to its credibility when its Bill was being discussed in Committee. According to one witness, speaking in his defence:

'I know from the experience of several sessions in connection with Mr Piercy and Mr Savin that it is always alleged by the opponents of any scheme to which those gentlemen are engineer and contractor that they are engaged in a number of projects of all sorts, and there is this curious circumstance connected with Mr Savin. We are told by one of our opponents that a few years ago he was a mercer in the town of Oswestry. If he was so, I say here, as I have had occasion to say before, that is only an additional proof of Mr Savin's skill in the business to which he has betaken himself, viz., that of making railways; but you will find, I have no doubt, in the course of this inquiry that here, as in other parts of Wales (I speak more especially of the North) the country would have remained unfurnished with railways unless Mr Savin had come to the rescue of the companies which were formed, and had applied the capital which he had accumulated, and applied what is of more importance, his energy, management, and skill, in making arrangements to get those companies out of their difficulties. I have no doubt that he will be asked here whether he is not connected to the extent of a large sum of money with the lines commonly called the 'Oswestry lines' up in North Wales, and with lines also extending from there in other directions. It is perfectly true that he has been, I admit that to be the truth, and I must admit it to be the truth that, but for his money, so far as I can judge, the greater part of Wales would have been left without railways; because I know some of the railways that were sanctioned as long ago as 1853 and 1854 were actually in inextricable difficulties for the want of application of the capital and skill of some such person as Mr Savin, from which they would never have escaped.'[18]

For WL Banks, who as Secretary of the Hereford, Hay, and Brecon Railway, had first hand knowledge of the man, Thomas Savin was a latter day George Stephenson: 'As the effort of one man, George Stephenson, in constructing the Rocket had been the means of entirely revolutionising the system of locomotion throughout England and elsewhere, so by the efforts chiefly of one man had railway communication spread throughout the Principality. Like Stephenson, he had begun low in the world, and what he had got he had obtained by his energy, perseverance, and industry, by honesty, rectitude, and unswerving business conduct.'[19]

The engineer at this time was Benjamin Piercy, formerly of Welshpool, but now of 28 Great George Street, London, SW 1. He had been the engineer of the Mid Wales Railway, and was able to report to the Kington and Eardisley directors in February 1863 that the working plans and sections for the line had been completed, and that everything was in readiness for the commencement of operations by the contractor directly he was put in possession of the land. One of those who been engaged in this preparatory work was the Radnorshire architect and surveyor, SW Williams, of Rhaeadr. He enjoyed WL Bank's confidence and with whom in June 1862 he walked from Bronllys 'the proposed new line from there to Talyllyn' and had £120 of shares in the Kington and Eardisley Railway. He had in fact left Benjamin Piercy's employment earlier in 1862 on February 29th to set up as a surveyor in his own right. The Revd James Davies was also very impressed by him and had supported his unsuccessful application in 1862 to become County Surveyor for Radnorshire.[20] It is not unlikely that Williams, the moral church builder, left Piercy, who had worked with Savin on the Mid Wales Railway, out of disapproval of his business methods, for 'the combination of Savin and Piercy was renowned for its habit of promoting lines at random without intending to make any and selling them to other parties after the

Acts had been obtained.'[21] Piercy completed the Bishop's Castle Railway after Savin for a lump sum of £25,000. The local resident engineer for the Kington and Eardisley line was to be Mr TD Roberts of Hay.

The first turf of the railway was cut at Kington in the Butts Meadows on Thursday, 12th March 1863 by the Right Honourable Jane Elizabeth Harley, Lady Langdale, 1796-1872, of Eywood in the parish of Titley, a house which was deemed to 'stand pre-eminent amid everything erected in this locality'. She was the first child of Edward, fifth earl of Oxford and Mortimer, and she married Henry Bickersteth,1783-1851, a lawyer who embraced medicine and was physician to Lady Oxford[22] before returning to the law and becoming Master of the Rolls and being ennobled as Lord Langdale. She was widowed in 1851 and there was one child from the marriage who married a Hungarian, Count Sangor Teleki, and thereby she came to play a modest part in European affairs. In the 1848 revolutions a friend of the count and countess, Lt General Lazar Meszaros, became Minister of National Defence and Supreme Commander of the Hungarian Army, but went into exile when the revolution failed. He came to England in 1851 and may have stayed at Eywood then, for in 1853 the Count and Countess Teleki were present with Lady Langdale at an assembly at Milner's Hotel. Later that year the General went on to the USA. He returned to England in 1858, a sick man, and he was nursed at Eywood with every attention by Lady Langdale and died there that year. He was buried in Titley churchyard where his stone was inscribed by 'his sorrowing friend JEH Lady Langdale.' Now regarded as a national hero, his body was returned to Hungary in 1991. Lady Langdale inherited extensive estates in 1853 on the death of her brother, Alfred, the sixth earl of Oxford and Mortimer, and the Kington and Eardisley Railway ran through her land at Titley. She died in Innsbruck in 1872 where she was buried.

Richard Parry, the Kington historian, and who purchased, he tells us, one ten pound share in the Kington and Eardisley Railway, left an eye witness account of the occasion: 'On this day a procession was formed at the Oxford Arms which proceeded to the ground accompanied by the band of the Kington Volunteers. A handsome lunch was prepared at the Oxford Arms Hotel by the order of Mr Savin of Shrewsbury, the spirited individual who first proposed the formation of the Kington and Eardisley Line of Railway and who advocated its construction in every stage of its proceeding to its accomplishment. The invitation to the luncheon extended to all shareholders in the neighbourhood. The tables were laid for 156 persons at the Oxford Arms. About 1,500 persons were in the Meadow to see the sod cut by Lady Langdale: it was a wet day and every person felt miserable and uncomfortable. The bells rang a merry peal and great rejoicing took place in the Town of Kington upon the Occasion.'[23]

The procession from the Oxford Arms consisted of:

A Body of Police
The Kington Volunteer Rifle Band in a carriage drawn by a pair of horses
Tradesmen and Gentlemen of the Town and Neighbourhood
The Directors
The Officers of the Company
Mr Sharpe, Hereford, the Contractor's Agent, bearing aloft the spade
Four navvies carrying the Wheelbarrow
Lady Langdale and the Chairman of the Company in her Ladyship's carriage
Mrs Davies, Moorcourt, and Mr RW Banks, Ridgebourne, in a carriage
Captain Peploe Webb and party in a carriage
Mr and Mrs Allen, of the Moor, and a party in a carriage.[24]

The solid silver and heavily chased spade, 'in the shape of a shield, the handle being polished oak, with a richly carved head and silver ring' had been specially made for the occasion. Like the wheelbarrow,'of polished oak, elaborately carved about the handles and the sides, and enriched with different devices', it had been manufactured, significantly at Brecon, the town the railway when complete was to make more accessible and which was already strongly represented on the board of directors. Indeed, the design of these objects was the work WL Banks himself, mayor of Brecon for 1859 and 1861. It was presented to Lady Langdale as a memento of the occasion and is now at Brampton Bryan Hall in the keeping of the Harley family. Unwilling to be eclipsed by Lady Langdale who 'had displayed all the skill of an experienced navigator', Sir Godfrey Morgan, WL Banks, James Davies, and Richard Banks all followed her example and in turn cut a sod and wheeled it away to the accompaniment of loud cheers.[25]

Amongst those not present at this auspicious occasion was James King-King, MP for the County and staunch opponent of the Kington and Eardisley Railway. Though invited, he was fortunate enough to have a previous engagement. His absence and that of the members for the county did not pass without comment. The chairman, Sir Godfrey Morgan, himself MP for Brecon, whilst assuring the company he had no doubt that genuine Parliamentary duties had kept them away from the proceedings, these self same duties had somehow or other evaded him that day. Another absentee was Richard Green Price. His sympathies at this stage were with the

Leominster and Kington and Lady Bateman who cut its first sod in 1854 had done the same service for the Knighton Railway in 1858 and Brassey and Field were the contractors for both railways.The Knighton Railway with which Green Price was so closely involved had opened in March 1861 and was now falteringly making its way to Llandrindod as the Central Wales Railway. Like James King-King, he had opposed the construction of the Kington and Eardisley, maintaining it had no local support and that it would be in unfair competition with his own line, the rails of which were alleged to be 'covered with rust for want of traffic.'

WL Banks had no doubts about the company's prospects. The Brecon and Merthyr line had been accomplished; the Hereford, Hay, and Brecon was fast approaching completion, both of which would place the Kington and Eardisley 'in direct communication with the great mineral district.' An extension to the Brecon and Merthyr line to Rumney would give access to Newport, and by another extension to Cardiff via Caerphilly. The Dulais Valley line could be extended to afford a direct line via Brecon to Neath and Swansea, whereas the Brecon Junction Railway would afford a direct link with Llandovery and Milford. Thus Kington, through this new railway, would have 'immediate communication with all the principal ports in South Wales...access to the populous districts of Merthyr and the Dulais Valley, which was one of the richest parts of South Wales,' And that was not all: the Kington and Eardisley intended to make its way to Craven Arms and would have by means of a second projected line direct access with 'the town of Birmingham.'[26]

He was equally confident about the company's financial prospects. He compared their position with that of Green Price's Central Wales Railway, in his opinion, their principal rival. The Central Wales had obtained its powers of extension in 1860 and according to its last half-yearly statement had expended upon it £8,901, of which sum £620 was a balance due at the bankers. On the other hand the latest half yearly statement of the Kington and Eardisley, only authorised in 1862, had spent more than double that sum, having purchased the Kington Tramway and had begun work on the line itself. Moreover they were breaking the local monopoly of the GWR and West Midland who had that year entered into an arrangement with the Leominster and Kington for working the line.

Unfortunately WL Banks lacked financial judgement just as much as he lacked judgement of character and many of the railways in which he was involved either never started services or soon went bankrupt when they did. The Neath and Brecon, for example, went bankrupt in 1866. Nor was he a good judge of a railway's potential viability. The Neath and Brecon was single track, steeply graded, and poorly built, and the Brecon and Merthyr had even more formidable terrain with which to contend. Restricted to single track and light trains, its purpose was to haul coal across the Brecon Beacons en route for Birkenhead and Birmingham, but it could never rival the lowland Newport-Hereford-Shrewsbury route.

A second Act was obtained by the Kington and Eardisley Railway in July 1864 by which time £15,698 had been received in shares and £15,520 spent on works, leaving only £178 in the bank. The engineer had been paid £1,100 and £79 had been spent on advertising. This second Act authorised seven deviations, including an extension from Lyonshall to Presteign, by-passing Kington. Another new line was proposed which was to run from Presteign to Nash, perhaps to serve the small quarries and lime kilns in the vicinity which may have been ripe for development, and with the ultimate intention of making its way to New Radnor. Several short connecting lines were also proposed to establish a complicated junction with the Leominster and Kington Railway. The long term intention of these revisions, besides giving access to Presteign, was to join the Knighton Railway at Bedstone, and if the Knighton Railway refused the Kington and Eardisley running powers, then it was proposed by a further act to lay down a duplicate track. The additional sums of money required were to be raised by £90,000 in shares and by borrowing a further £30,000.

NOTES

1. Banks Archive.
2. HT 5.4.1862.
3. H Miles, J.P., of Downfield, High Sheriff of Radnorshire in 1847; W Deykes, Castlefield House, Church Street Kington; the vicar of Kington, the Revd H Whateley; the headmaster of the Grammar School, the Revd J N Walsh.
4. Benjamin Bodenham, A Cheese, E Cheese, and T S Rogers.
5. James Pugh. He was also Clerk to the local Justices and to the Commissioner of Taxes.
6. E B Price. He was manager of the Kington and Radnorshire Bank.
7. Thomas Price, who was also Clerk to the Turnpike Trustees and a banker's clerk.
8. eg Mr J M Milner, the proprietor of the Burton Hotel; Mr Ferrier of Malhollam, farmer, and a former tenant of James Watt at Stonehouse, Gladestry, and Mr E Vaughan, the Kington currier who had been so active in the early stages of the Leominster and Kington Railway.
9. See Table I.
10. Pevsner, N, *The Buildings of England: Shropshire*, Harmondsworth, 1958. p.171.
11. Ferryside, near Carmarthen.
12. The Sheriffs was purchased by the Revd James Davies to become part of his Moorcourt estate.
13. HT 5.4.1862.

14. Of Penybont Hall, Radnorshire.
15. HT 5.4.1862.
16. Ibid.
17. HT 14.3.1863.
18. HT 5.4.1862.
19. Ibid.
20. Davies wrote to him two days later to commiserate: 'You created a very favourable impression and had a fair amount of support.' For an account of S W Williams, see Fenn, R W D , and Sinclair, J B, "Our Ubiquitous Friend', S W Williams, FSA, FRIBA, 1837-1899', TRS, LIX, 1989, pp.116-133.
21. Baughan,P.E., *North and Mid Wales*, Vol.11, A Regional History of the Railways of Great Britain, Newton Abbot, 1980, p.53.
22. Dr Mitchell, one of the Tramway proprietors, was also one of her appointments.
23. FRRP p.8.
24. The presence of Mr and Mrs Allen of the Moor, Lyonshall, is interesting. In 1840 Charles William Allen, JP, was in dispute with the proprietors of the Tramway over its fences through his estate. The Company had made a cash settlement instead of fences with the previous owner and after some acrimonious open letters in the *Hereford Times* Mr Allen brought an action against the Company which he won, being awarded £37 11s 4d, the cost of the fences made by him. The dispute was obviously now forgotten. He assumed the surname Greenly in 1866 and thereby illustrates the frequency with which surnames were changed by the Victorians, to the confusion of later historians; the Reverend James Davies of Moorcourt was, of course, originally the Reverend James Banks.
25. HT 14.3.1863.
26. Ibid.

TABLE

Pedigree illustrating the Penson architectural dynasty

Thomas Penson, Senior, 1760-1859
County Surveyor of Flintshire

|

Thomas Penson, Junior, 1791-1859
County Surveyor of Monts & Denbs

Richard Kyrke Penson, 1816-1886   Thomas Mainwearing Penson, 1818-1864
Followed father as County Sur-   Church & Domestic Architect
veyor of Montgomeryshire.
Director of the Kington and
Eardisley, Bishop's Castle,
Buckley, Hoylake, Wrexham,
and Connah's Quay Railways

CHAPTER FIVE: THE KINGTON & EARDISLEY RAILWAY II

A ll was now not well with the shareholders of the Kington and Eardisley Railway Company and in November 1864 a *Memorial* was presented to the directors of the Company, signed by thirty-five shareholders, including Richard and RW Banks, the vicar of Lyonshall; Anthony Temple, a Kington lawyer; and Henry Meredith:

'We the undersigned inhabitants of Kington and the neighbourhood being promoters and shareholders of the original line of Railway from Eardisley to Kington have observed with great regret a notice in the Hereford papers purporting to be signed by the Solicitors of this Company of an intended application to Parliament in the next Session for an Act to authorise the extension of the lines authorised by the Kington and Eardisley Acts of 1862 and 1864 from Presteign to Llangunllo.

The line of Railway contemplated by the first Act was from the tramway of the Kington Railway Company in Kington to the Hereford, Hay, and Brecon Railway in the Parish of Eardisley with a branch line to join the Leominster and Kington Railway at Marston and in furtherance of this line of railway and on the faith of the assurance of Mr Savin that he would make the line we took shares and executed the subscription contract.

With a view to extend the operation of the Railway and make it as beneficial as possible to the proposed Contractor an extension of the Railway from Marston to the Craven Arms with a branch line to Presteign was applied for in the Session of 1863 and was successfully opposed by the London and North Western Company. We viewed this opposition with much regret as it entailed considerable expense on Mr Savin, delayed the commencement of the authorised line and gave rise to another application in the Session of Parliament of 1864 for an extension from Marston to Presteign at the instance as we are informed of an active opponent of the Bill of the previous Session.

It is our belief that the further extension now proposed from Presteign to Llangunllo is uncalled for by the wants of the country through which it will pass, that it is not desired by the shareholders or the inhabitants of Kington and Presteign and that if such an extension is authorised it will be such an encumbrance on the authorised lines as to deter any contractor from undertaking their execution.

We are unable to learn that any progress has been made either in the actual purchase of lands or otherwise on the authorised lines and we therefore submit that it is desirable that the authorised lines shall be commenced and completed before any further extensions are sanctioned by your Board.

We trust that our representations may have their due effect and we think it well thus early to intimate that we shall oppose to the utmost of our power the Bill which is intended to be applied for if it is brought in.'[1]

The immediate cause of the alarm which generated this *Memorial* was, no doubt, the Radnorshire Railways Bill of 1865 which proposed a line from Presteign to Llangunllo where it would join the Central Wales Railway and travel to Llandinam to join the Cambrian Railways. The Bill was, in fact, withdrawn, but the Lugg Valley Railway Bill, joining Presteign to Llangunllo, did get the Royal Assent, though it was never implemented. Its authorised capital was of £90,000 in shares and £30,000 on loan and it secured running arrangements not only with the Kington and Eardisley Railway, but also with the Leominster and Kington, the Central Wales, and the Great Western Railways. The chairman of its directors was Richard Green Price. A year later, the Knighton Railway, another Green Price enterprise, unsuccessfully promoted a bill for a branch line to Presteign. Had all these ventures flourished, Presteign's economic development would have been immensely enhanced to Kington's cost, for the two towns had always been rivals and it had long been apparent that due to their proximity one could only flourish at the expense of the other.

Also in 1865 the Kington and Eardisley Railway had to obtain a third Act, this time to authorise the Company to divide the shares in its capital into deferred and preferred half-shares, no doubt in an attempt to promote the company's flagging powers of attraction for investment. But three years after the Company's inception no trains had yet been run and the track which was commenced from the Eardisley end was still far from complete.

In February 1866 Savin, who at one stage in his career was a millionaire, ceased trading and went bankrupt and his £16,000 worth of ordinary shares in the Kington and Eardisley were sold. Daniel Climie was appointed in his place as contractor in July 1864, but he also went bankrupt, in the following May. Savin, thereupon, tendered again in June 1865 and in May 1867 Thomas Evans, of Newport, took over for a year and further legislation was obtained in 1868. This authorised the company to make some deviations at Titley and at Presteign where it was now proposed to join the Lugg Valley and Bishop's Castle Railways as anticipated, at least in part, by those who signed the 1864 *Memorial*. It also empowered the Company to use a portion of the Leominster and Kington Railway's line between Titley and Kington. Mr TD Roberts, now of Brecon, is named as the sole engineer. But actual work on the track did not start again until 1872 when Charles Chambers of Gravel Hill, Kington, and Westminster, took over as contractor and completed the line.

There were other changes too besides those involving contractors and legislation. By 1869 WL Banks, now a JP, had become chairman of the company, and, rather more surprisingly, Richard Green Price, MP since 1863 for the Radnorshire boroughs, appears as vice-chairman. Banks's fortunes were were failing due mainly to a succession of unsuccessful railway speculations and, according to family legend, were only rescued by his second marriage, in 1867, to Elizabeth Maria Richards, of Ynys in Anglesey. He moved to North Wales where he had a succession of homes and acquired new and perhaps less costly interests: freemasonry, antiquarianism, and the Royal Cambrian Academy.

As a freemason he achieved the craft's highest position in North Wales, that of Past Senior Grand Warden of North Wales. Elected an FSA, his enthusiasm for antiquarian subjects did not run to paying his annual subscription to the Society, and for this reason he was removed from Fellowship in 1873. He was also an enthusiastic founder-member of the Royal Cambrian Academy, established in 1881, and served first as its honorary secretary and then as its treasurer, playing an important part in the restoration of its famous Elizabethan headquarters at Plas Mawr, Conway. The railway, however, never entirely lost its hold upon him, and in North Wales, besides retaining his interest in the Hereford, Hay, and Brecon Railway, he took up directorships in the Denbigh, Ruthin, and Corwen Railway, on which SW Williams had worked as a surveyor, and the Whitby, Redcar, and Middlesbrough Union Railway. He died in January 1893 at his Conway home after a long illness terminating in paralysis.

Another new name on the board of directors was that of Stephen Robinson, JP. Born in 1829 in Yorkshire where he was educated at Richmond Grammar School, he settled at Lynhales in the parish of Lyonshall where he farmed 430 acres. He was also a director of the Brecon and Merthyr Tydfil Junction Railway and the Pembroke and Tenby Railway. He was prominent in county affairs, being High Sheriff of Herefordshire in 1871 and a Deputy Lieutenant of the county. He became an alderman in 1889 and from 1887-1906 was chairman of the Kington Board of Guardians. The Kington and

Eardisley Railway ran through his land at Lyonshall where it also adjoined the new station with its single 200ft platform. He acquired 1,100 shares in the Company in the early days of 1862 and by 1873 his holding amounted to 24,100.

Yet another Act was obtained in June 1871 whereby the Presteign extension was abandoned and the main line was varied at several places with the consent of landowners, 'the better to accommodate their wants and the requirements of the district.' Running powers over the Leominster and Kington Railway between Titley and Kington were granted by an agreement of April 1868 with that Company and the Great Western Railway.

The contract the Company entered into with Charles Chambers was for the completion of the line for £32,000 in cash and £2,000 in ordinary shares. The work was to be finished within eighteen months of receiving a month's notice from the company's engineer to proceed, and there was a penalty clause for not completing the contract on time. A year later it was reported that the work from Eardisley to Titley had been steadily progressing throughout the summer and that this portion of the line was capable of being wholly prepared for the visit of the Government inspector. It was hoped that this would take place at an early date and that the line would be opened forthwith. Notwithstanding the strenuous opposition of the Hereford, Hay, and Brecon Railway, no longer modified in its thinking by WL Banks, its former secretary, full powers were obtained under the Act to run into and use the Eardisley station. It was further reported to the shareholders that arrangements had been concluded and an agreement entered into with the GWR for the working of the original and the extension lines and it was expected that those lines would ensure to them a good and improving profit.

Francis Lewis Bodenham, of Castle Street, Hereford, was now chairman of the Company, and his family, with its strong legal traditions, had several railway connections, one of which was with the Kington Tramway. He himself, besides being a solicitor, was Treasurer for the county of Hereford, and had directorships in the Newport, Abergavenny, and Hereford Railway, the Worcester, Bromyard, and Leominster Railway, of which one of his fellow directors was Richard Green Price, the West Midland Railway, and the Great Western Railway itself, though he had retired from the latter by 1872.

In 1874 the possibility of a westward extension from Kington was raised once again in the form of the proposed Worcester and Aberystwyth Junction

Railway. An Act was obtained authorising the line to continue from the Kington and Eardisley Railway at New Radnor to Rhaeadr and then to join the Manchester and Milford near Llangurig. Dansey Green Price complained bitterly about the lack of support for the venture, especially around Penybont, where the line was to cross the Central Wales line. The Revd Sir Gilbert Lewis, of Harpton Court, who since 1862 had £1,000 of debentures in the Kington and Eardisley Company and had just acquired a further £3,900 in preference shares, took up £1,000 worth of shares in the new Company. However, he stipulated he would only contribute more if his debentures in the Kington and Eardisley were redeemed at par.

The Worcester and Aberystwyth scheme was modified in 1877 by moving its proposed terminus from Rhaeadr to Builth, and Dansey Green Price wrote again to Sir Gilbert, who replied with some impatience, the troubles of the Leominster and Kington, of which he was now a director, in general and with the Green Prices in particular, being fresh in his mind: 'It is a matter of indifference to myself whether the line goes to Rhaeadr or Builth; I have had enough of railway making and will decline again to take shares.' The hopes of the line remained unfulfilled and the company was wound up in 1880.

The Kington and Eardisley Railway, however, owned the remaining portion of the Tramway from Sunset Wharf to Burlingjobb and had kept it open in accordance with their 1862 Act. But they were under no obligation to replace it with a normal railway. The inconvenience, though, of transferring all traffic at Kington from one gauge to another, and the increasing output of the lime works were responsible for the decision to construct a full-sized railway from Kington to New Radnor and which would run parallel with the old railway for part of the distance. Plans for the new railway were deposited with the Quarter Sessions in November 1872.

The necessary legislation for the New Radnor Railway was completed in June 1873 whereby the construction was authorised of a line, six and a half miles in length, joining the Leominster and Kington at Kington. The connection with the Kington and Eardisley Railway, of whose system the line was to be part, resumed at Titley on the Leominster and Kington line. The Kington and Eardisley Railway was empowered to raise new capital of £60,000 in shares and £20,000 in loans. It was confidently believed that the new line was for the most part of easy construction and 'will in all probability be completed during the summer of 1874.' It was also reported that the directors[2] were actively negotiating for the funds they needed to complete all the preliminary works and to proceed immediately with the new line. Perhaps with unfounded optimism they confessed they had what they believed to be well founded hopes of being able to obtain all the funds they needed on reasonable terms. Meanwhile, Colonel Hutchinson, for the Board of Trade, inspected the Kington to Eardisley line in July 1874, and though he required the layout of Almeley station to be altered, he gave his approval for the line to be brought into service. The public opening took place on August 3rd 1874, an official party travelling with luncheon baskets by the 12. 20 pm from Kington for an al fresco lunch in a field adjoining Eardisley station. The return trip conveyed Mr Justice Quain en route for Presteign assizes.

Between Titley and Almeley the line dropped 300ft in 3 miles at gradients varying between 1 in 44 and 1 in 47. This was steep; 1 in 70 is thought a good main line gradient. The very steep Lickey Incline in Worcestershire is 1 in 35, that out of Exeter 1 in 37, and out of Euston at Bow Road 1 in 40. The Cowlairs incline out of Glasgow's Queen Street is 1 in 41/50 and the trains leaving the station were once assisted with wire ropes. The Kington and Eardisley stations, none of which afforded their stationmasters any accommodation, were architecturally modest which is perhaps surprising bearing in mind SW Williams's connection with the line, for he is suspected of having had a hand in the design of Llanidloes station, a handsome building indeed. Not only were the Kington and Eardisley line's stations spartan in their passenger amenities, it was also often said that they lacked adequate loading facilities for goods traffic. The line was unusual as well in that it had no signal boxes, the signals being entirely operated by ground frames.

On August 14th 1875 the *Hereford Times* reported that 'the line from Kington to New Radnor was inspected and passed on Friday last by Colonel Hutchinson on behalf of the Board of Trade. He expressed himself highly pleased with the way in which the works were finished. This line, a portion of the Kington and Eardisley Railway, will eventually become part of a system of railways from Worcester and Aberystwyth for which the Acts have been obtained. Mr G Wells Owen, of Westminster, is the engineer and Mr Charles Chambers, London SW1, is the contractor.' Charles Chambers was the contractor for two other railway ventures with Dansey Green Price: the Golden Valley Railway, in which he was helped by his sons Walter and Herbert, and the Shropshire Railways, 1889-91. He and Walter were also directors of the Southwold Railway, in East Anglia.

Once again the railway buildings were austere and the terminus at New

Radnor certainly did not *look* like a terminus; it had only a single platform, its station buildings and goods shed were architecturally insignificant and there was no stationmaster's house. Trackwise, it only had a run around loop and a solitary siding. Inconveniently sited at the foot of Smatcher Hill, it was half a mile from the town where the stationmaster had his house in Broad Street. Dolyhir had a single platform, a passing loop, a private siding for Lord Ormathwaite's Strinds Quarry, and a siding for the Old Radnor Trading Company. Stanner also had one platform and one siding.

A poster celebrated the opening of the New Radnor extension on September 25th 1875. An event which, it announced, would be 'celebrated at New Radnor by the distribution of a Fat Ox to the deserving Poor resident within a mile and a half of the Town Hall, New Radnor. Tea will also be provided for the Women and Children. Athletic Sports will take place in a field near the Station: also a Grand Display of Fireworks in the Evening. A Brass Band will be in attendance. Public Luncheon at the Eagle Hotel, New Radnor at Two O'Clock.'

On the day 'a procession was formed, headed by a band, the members of the Oddfellows Club with banners, the Sunday Schools, members of all clubs and institutions, visitors and tradesmen and a gaily decorated wagon containing a fine ox, two other wagons containing dressed sheep and bread and several wagons of coals for distribution to the poor.' The menu for the official luncheon was:

	Boiled Beef	
Ducks	Plain Lobster	Lamb
Green Goose		Turkey Poults
	Haunch of Mutton	
Mayonnaise of Chicken		Tongues of Ham
Roast Fowls		Lobster Salad
	Sirloin of Ribs of Beef	
Bachamat Chicken		Marble Veal
Game Pie	Partridges	Giblet Pie
	Tarts	
Cuacoa Jelly		Cheese Cakes
Grapes	Nuts	Apples[3]

Sir Richard Green Price had, once again, invested heavily in the construction of the New Radnor Railway, and, according to Charles Chambers, the line would never have been built had Sir Richard and his son

Dansey not taken up £50,000 in share capital and debentures. 'Who else but he,' asked Richard Green Price's son Dansey in a letter to the *Hereford Times* in December 1889, 'could have carried through the Presteign and New Radnor lines, guaranteeing large sums of money, only to find in the latter case that the Great Western Railway broke their promises, and withdrew their agreement at the end of five years?' Sir Dansey Green Price renewed his complaint at the unveiling of his father's memorial obelisk on the hill above Norton in 1907, wishing the GWR had kept faith in regard to the Kington and Eardisley line, for if they had done so the line would be going through the country to Aberystwyth. But the line stood still at New Radnor, although he hoped it was not destined to do so for ever.

But in November 1876 the Company's directors, Richard Green Price, Stephen Robinson, CW Greenly, Hubert EF Lewis, and EH Greenly, had to write to the 460 Kington and Eardisley's shareholders: 'Notwithstanding the most strenuous efforts and great personal pecuniary sacrifice on our part, the complications arising from the unsatisfactory financial condition of the Company compelled us to seriously consider what steps could be taken to preserve your property from becoming a prey to litigation.'[4] The statement went on to inform the shareholders that the Company had insufficient capital to complete its lines and liabilities to landowners amounting to some £800 and other liabilities of £43,000. There was perhaps some eccentricity in the way some, at least, of the directors conducted their affairs for the company. For example, in 1876 the company was still acquiring land, some of which came from EH Greenly for which he was paid £500 in cash and £350 in debenture stock: he in turn bought some surplus Tramway land from the company. The appropriate deed of conveyance was rather casually witnessed for Greenly by 'William Griffiths, Gardner (sic) to EH Greenly.'

Since August 1875 the line had been worked by the GWR by an agreement which was renewable in 1880. By this agreement the company 'was obliged to execute certain additional works' which if it failed to undertake the GWR could carry out and deduct their cost from the revenues taken on the line. However, without reconstituting the entire financial structure of the company it was feared that 'anarchy and litigation cannot be avoided and in that event it will inevitably be years before the mortgages receive any payment whatsoever.'[5]

Basically, the Company lacked vigour and its shareholders were only with difficulty persuaded to concern themselves with its affairs. Thus, George Sneath, the Company secretary, wrote in February 1884 from the Company's Gresham Street office in the City to John Gwynne James, a

Hereford solicitor: 'In case you should not be able to attend the forthcoming meeting, I enclose a form of Proxy which please sign, in the presence of a witness, and return to me. We have some difficulty in obtaining the presence of the necessary number of Shareholders or I would not trouble you.'[6]

By 1888 Stephen Robinson was Company chairman and Sir Richard Dansey Green Price had joined the board in place of his father who had died the previous year. Charles Chambers had also joined the board. The GWR was still working the line, as it had from its opening, and was taking 50% of the gross receipts. In 1890 the Kington and Eardisley Railway Company invited Mr Arthur Pain, MInstCE, of 12 Victoria Street, SW1, to make a report on the Company. His brief was to examine and report on the line's present state of repair; to examine the feasibility of the Company working the line itself; the costs involved; the probable amount of traffic; and the cost of providing the necessary rolling stock and engines.[7]

Arthur Pain came to Kington in January 1890 and spent three days in the 'careful inspection' of the railway with the assistance of Mr Walter Chambers 'who having constructed the Railway under his father was enabled to give... much valuable information.' He also studied the Parliamentary Acts of 1862, 1864, 1865, 1868, 1873, and 1875 concerning the Company and the agreements made with the GWR in 1873, 1875, 1885, and 1887. In his report he notes that some four miles of the permanent way, out of the six miles seven furlongs and two chains of the total length of the Eardisley section, had been entirely removed. The surviving rails which were insufficiently ballasted, were second-hand 'having been previously turned and well worn on other parts of the Great Western system.' The New Radnor section was also insufficiently ballasted.

Now, in the opinion of Mr Pain, article eight of the Company's working agreement with the GWR excluded the use of old materials in repairs and renewals, all of which were new when the GWR commenced working the line. The cost of renewing this track would have to be met by the Kington and Eardisley were it to take over the running of the line. As to the feasibility of the Company doing this, Mr Pain was very doubtful, since 'the line is not favourably situated for being worked independently, it being practically in two separate sections. The Great Western Company as the working company under a long lease of the Leominster and Kington Railway hold the connecting link between the Eardisley and New Radnor sections of your Railway, namely the 1¼ miles between Kington and Titley. The result might be that the Great Western could put such obstacles in the way of running the train service and the tolls and rates for the traffic, that your Company would be seriously hampered in the conduct of the traffic.'

This situation, of course, could have been disputed in court, but again the Company would have been involved in heavy expenses with no guarantee of a successful outcome. Another problem was that the bulk of the traffic on the Kington and Eardisley line eventually went to stations on the Great Western. As to the cost of working the line, Mr Pain concluded that 'the heavy gradients and sharp curves increase the cost of working as regards wear and tear and consumption of fuel. Assuming that the Engines and Rolling Stock are your own property and that the Great Western Company put the line in thorough repair, I am of the opinion that it will cost you £2,830 a year, exclusive of the Secretary's salary and expenses.'

The gross receipts for the previous year, ending in June 1889, amounted to £3,870, or £5 10s per mile per week. These receipts were unlikely to increase very much, 'although a close alliance with the Midland Company would very much help you.... The least amount of stock with which the line could be worked would be Two Tank Engines of 30 Tons, fitted with steam brakes, Four composite carriages, Two brake vans, Five low sided Trucks, Two box Wagons, and one Travelling crane. These I estimate would cost £6,000. I think you may assume that the Great Western & Midland Companies would provide you with the rest of the low sided Trucks, Cattle Trucks, and Timber Wagons required for traffic consigned over their systems.'

The Company owed the Great Western £5,190 and Mr Pain thought the latter 'will require the payment of this sum if terms cannot be arranged for their continuing to work the line.' Consequently his advice was that 'if possible the Great Western should be induced to continue to work the line on the present terms if possible for a term not exceeding five years.' A condition of renewing the lease would be that the Great Western renewed all structures and permanent way with new materials, and the lease should not be renewed for a longer term than five years, 'for I believe that the growing prosperity of the country may cause fresh extensions of the Railways in that district which would tend to improve your property and enable you to make better terms with the Great Western or some other Company.'

Contrary to Pain's judgement, it was said by those who originally proposed the six miles of the Kington and Eardisley that 'the gradients are most easy, there are no viaducts or long bridges, and scarcely any heavy cutting of earthworks.'[8] In 1862 WL Banks had argued before the Parliamentary committee that the works could be completed for something under £84,000 which would give an average cost of £9,000 per mile. 'It had been clearly proved by railway statistics that lines constructed at a cost not exceeding £10,000 a mile paid dividends of 5% or upwards, even in agricultural districts; so that upon the most reliable data, there was every prospect of the line paying a good dividend.'

In 1889 amongst those expecting a good dividend were several institutions; the London Financial Association, Ltd., the Lancashire Insurance Company, the National Bank of Scotland, the Worcester City and County Bank, the Devon and Cornwall Bank, Plymouth, all of which were qualified by the size of their investment to nominate a candidate each to stand for election to the board of directors. Other shareholding institutions were the Midland Land and Investment Co., Ltd., the Manchester Fire Assurance Co., The Railways and General Company, Ltd., and the Hibernian Joint Stock Company, of Dublin. The company never had its own rolling stock or locomotives, so one wonders why the Ashbury Railway Carriage and Iron Company, Ltd., of Manchester, and the Midland Railway Carriage and Wagon Company, of Birmingham, both had sufficient shares to stand for the board. Perhaps such concerns as Vickers Sons and Co, Ltd., of Sheffield; Arthur Keen of the Patent Nut and Bolt Co., of Birmingham; the Boyne Engine Works, of Hunslet, Leeds; the Ebbw Vale Steel, Iron, and Coal Co., Ltd.; the Bryndu Colliery of Bridgend, Glamorgan; and the Great Western Railway had some indirect interest in the company's affairs, perhaps even being paid in kind for previous services.[9]

Amongst individual subscribers, the biggest category was of those described as gentlemen or esquires, of whom there were 185, besides three peers of the realm, five baronets, and a knight. The next largest category consisted of forty-three farmers, followed by thirty-five spinsters, twenty widows, nineteen clerks in holy orders, and fifteen lawyers. There was also a spade tree maker, a watchmaker, a gardener, and a gaoler. One hundred and six shareholders lived in London; seventy-one in Kington; fifty-four in Presteign; and thirty-eight in Manchester. Four lived in Ireland; four lived in Guernsey; two on the Isle of Wight; and one in Penzance.[10]

In some respects it is surprising that the extended Kington and Eardisley Railway did not pay a good dividend because, if for no other reason, of the traffic generated by the Old Radnor Trading Company through Dolyhir station. Its management was closely linked with that of the Kington and Eardisley Railway and in the year 1884-5, for example, consignments went by rail from Dolyhir to:

Almeley	Leominster
Bacton	Lyonshall
Bilston	Moorhampton
Cradley	Newbridge on Wye
Credenhill	Oswestry
Dinmore	Pembridge
Doldowlod	Penybont
Eardisley	Rhaeadr
Hay	St Harmon's
Kinnersley	Steen's Bridge
Kingsland	Woofferton
Knighton	Worcester

That same financial year £1872 2s 10d was paid to the GWR; £520 5s 7d to the Midland Railway; and £78 13s 3d to the Mid Wales Railway. Much of the traffic generating these payments travelled to and from either Dolyhir or Kington and a substantial proportion of it would have arrived through the Railways Clearing House at the bank account of the Kington and Eardisley Railway. In the financial year 1889-90 the Old Radnor Trading Company had depots at the railway stations at Hereford, Woofferton, Steen's Bridge, Leominster, Kingsland, Pembridge, Presteign, New Radnor, Dolyhir, Kington, Lyonshall, Moorhampton, Kinnersley, Eardisley, Whitney, Hay, and Glasbury. The existence of these agencies in a commercial enterprise, with coal stocks of £6442 0s 4d, all arriving by rail, together with payments of £1107 13s 4d for the hire of wagons, and £3724 11s 7d paid in railway carriage, all imply that a considerable amount of revenue producing goods traffic passed over the metals of the Kington and Eardisley Railway.[11]

In the end, the line had proved to be very expensive to make and its subscribed capital, to which must be added £1,500 lent by the Great Western Railway, totalled no less than £263,459 for a mere thirteen miles. The lease was renewed with the Great Western in 1890 and they bought it outright for £45,000 in July 1897 when, after a history of thirty-five years, it went into liquidation, Walter Chambers, who had helped his father in completing the line, being one of the liquidators. The bargain was a poor one for the shareholders: the maximum payment to debenture holders was £62 10s for each £100 share whilst the ordinary shares of the same value were purchased for £2, both classes being fully paid up. The final shareholders' meeting was held at twelve noon on Tuesday, 12th July 1898, at the Company's London office at 44 Gresham Street, 'for the purpose of passing formal resolutions closing the Liquidation.'

The issue of the westward extension of the line from New Radnor came up yet again in 1898 when, with others, SW Williams promoted the East and West Wales Railway Bill which was intended to fulfil the intentions of the aborted Worcester and Aberystwyth Junction Railway by building a line from New Radnor via Penybont to Rhaeadr. From Rhaeadr this time it would travel along the Wye Valley to just south of Llangurig from whence it would make its way to Aberystwyth by a similar route to that of the Manchester and Milford. It was, no doubt, through the influence of Williams, who had been county surveyor for many years, that the Radnorshire County Council considered how it might help in its construction. The problems, however, presented by the Radnor Forest once again proved insuperable and the project did not proceed.

When the GWR opened its Fishguard harbour in 1909 the westward extension from New Radnor was yet again discussed. This time the line would have run south of the Radnor Forest, across the Central Wales line at Llandrindod and over the Mid Wales near Newbridge on Wye to join the Manchester and Milford on this occasion between Tregaron and Lampeter. A new line would link Newcastle Emlyn to Goodwick. As a consequence it was believed 'the great population of the Midlands could take advantage of the shorter sea route to Ireland.' Significantly a photograph of Dolyhir station in 1910 shows a large advertisement on the wall of the station building urging passengers: 'Go by the new Fishguard route to Ireland', no doubt anticipating the day when the latest new route would be via New Radnor.

An article in the *Railway Magazine* in 1910 discussed the merits of the new route:

'The object of the scheme, presumably, would be to provide a fairly direct and alternative route from the Great Western Railway's new ocean port to the populous Midlands and North Midlands, and would even give an alternative route to London, if needed, in an emergency. As showing the wonderful ubiquity of the Great Western Railway, although the distance is over 260 miles, such an alternative route would not touch the present route, except the last 52 miles from Didcot and would not be so very much longer.

Apart from its alleged chief object such a railway would serve numerous small interests. To mention one, there is the rapidly rising and popular Welsh inland spa of Llandrindod Wells, badly in need of a direct approach (sic!) and there is every reason to believe it might rival

Harrogate and Buxton, if better placed in regard of railway facilities. The present route to Llandrindod Wells is a most roundabout journey to this fashionable and populous centre.'[12]

The rumours of a new route continued until the outbreak of the Great War in 1914.

Those who originally promoted the Kington and Eardisley Railway committed three serious errors of judgement which prevented the line from ever fulfilling their expectations. The original plan of a separate terminus at Kington should have been adhered to. This would have obviated the need to run over another company's metals. This was only for a mile and a quarter, but it made the Company a permanent hostage to fortune and when the New Radnor extension opened gave rise to the ludicrous situation of a single company running a railway in two separate parts. Secondly, the layout at Titley Junction worked to the disadvantage of the Kington and Eardisley by preventing direct access to Leominster and the north. Lastly, the Company should have sought closer relations with the Midland Company rather than with the Great Western, for it was through the Midland's Brecon and Hay line that it have had commercially invaluable links with South Wales.

NOTES

1. PRO RAIL 336/20.
2. Who at this time were: Benjamin Bodenham, of 1 Castle Street, Hereford, chairman; the Revd Sir GF Lewis, of Harpton Court; Charles William Greenly, of Titley Court; Capt Corbett, of Greenfields, Presteign; Richard Green Price, of Norton Manor; and Stephen Robinson, of Lynhales, Lyonshall.
3. Quoted by Guy Chambers, whose grandfather Charles Chambers, assisted by his two sons, Walter and Herbert, was engineer of the New Radnor and Presteign extensions as well as of the completion of the Kington and Eardisley Railway. ('Astonishing story of the quarries of Old Radnor, *The Quarry Managers' Journal*, October 1958, p. 128.)
4. PRO RAIL 336/5.
5. Ibid.
6. Correspondence in the possession of the authors.
7. PRO RAIL 336/6.
8. HT 14.3.1863.
9. PRO RAIL 336/8.
10. Ibid.
11. Old Radnor Trading Company, Trading Account Book, No 1, deposited with Kington Museum.
12. Husband, J F,'Some Border Bye-ways of the Great Western Railway', *Railway Magazine*, March, 1910, p. 190.

CHAPTER 6: THE IMPACT OF THE RAILWAY.

In April 1862, speaking at a public meeting at the Oxford Arms, Kington, to promote the Kington and Eardisley Railway, the local lawyer and the town's elder statesman, Richard Banks, recollected that in the winter it had once taken him five and a half hours travelling from Kington to Leominster 'in a post chaise with a pair of good horses and not a scrap of luggage.'[1] Now, at least according to the time-table, it could be done in the fastest train of the day, the 11.45, in thirty-five minutes and it could be done in relative safety and comfort. The *Hereford Journal*, for example, had reported on the 12th August 1822 that 'as James Davies, Esqr., and Richard Banks, Esqr., were returning to Kington from Shrewsbury Assizes the horse took fright near Longer and both gentlemen were thrown out of the carriage. Mr Banks escaped with trifling injury but Mr Davies was seriously hurt. The numerous friends of this respected gentleman will feel gratified to learn that he is rapidly recovering.' On the other hand, trains with corridors throughout were not introduced in Britain until 1892 and such carriages always remained rare on the Kington lines. Perhaps the *ABC Railway Guide* of 1859, when it advertised on its front page 'The Deane Harding Automatic Revolver, the most simple in construction,' had more in mind than the anxieties of the nervous.

The coming of the railway to the district transformed local life, enriching the cultural as well as the material prosperity of the area. Thus in 1863 for the first time the Cambrian Archaeological Association was able to hold its annual summer meeting that year at Kington because of its railway connections with the rest of the county. The Woolhope Club, which had visited Llandrindod Wells on a day excursion by rail in 1867, came by train to Dolyhir in 1888 to inspect the quarries. They first visited the Old Radnor Trading Company's quarries, facing the station, and were conducted around the site by Mr CW Lloyd, the manager. They then crossed the railway to see the quarries of Messrs Field and Co, where we are told they observed an early use of 'gelatine-dynamite for blasting.' The Club returned again in 1928 when they saw the lime kilns in action.

In its early days the railway was often, especially when it ran on Sundays, seen as a serious hindrance to Godly living, but not so at Kington. In 1859 the attendance at Mr Onions' temperance meetings, held in Kington at Milner's Assembly Room, amounted to some six hundred people, all taking tea, of course, and for whom 'special railway accommodation was provided at a low price for visitors from Hereford and Leominster.'[2]

Within a few years of its opening the Leominster and Kington Railway was offering tourists tickets to places hitherto quite inaccessible to the local population. One could now go, for example, to Llandudno and back for 23s and in 1862 a four day excursion to London for ten shillings. 'Ireland, the lakes of Cumberland and Westmoreland, and the watering places of the Lancashire coast' all became available on special tourist tickets, valid for a month. Day returns were available to Chester, Birkenhead, Liverpool, Manchester, Wolverhampton, and Birmingham. A day at Cheltenham races in 1914 or in 1963, 'on less than 2d a mile cost' one could have a day in Scotland, going to Fort William, a road trip to Glencoe and a steamer cruise on Loch Linnhe, all for £5 10 inclusive.

Tuesday Market tickets were introduced for Kington from the surrounding villages at one and threepence return from Eardisley, a shilling return from Presteign, Almeley, and New Radnor, and sixpence from Dolyhir, Stanner, and Lyonshall. Attempts, however, by the farming community to get Market tickets in the opposite direction, that is from Kington to Leominster, were resisted by the GWR. Season tickets were also available though few seem to have availed themselves of the facility. The Register of Season Ticket Agreements between Presteign and Kington has only two entries, both second class, for the period January 1878 to March 1884, though the quarterly second class fare remained the same, £3 2s 9d.

The railway made seaside holidays popular though one still needed considerable stamina for the journey. Moreover, the stage coach was not immediately displaced. Aberystwyth acquired a railway in 1858, but the stage coach still offered the quickest way there from Kington and its new railway was seen as a source of further revenue for the coach's proprietors who advertised in the *Hereford Times* in May 1859 that the pleasures of sea bathing were now only a mere eight and a half hours away, a vast improvement on the fifteen hours it took at the turn of the century before the roads were improved. 'The Cambrian Coach will commence running between Kington and Aberystwyth daily, Sundays excepted, for the Summer Season on Wednesday, June 1st, leaving the Oxford Arms Hotel and the Railway Station, Kington, immediately after the arrival of the 11.30 train, arriving at Belle Vue and the Gogerddan Arms, Aberystwyth, at 7.30, returning from Aberystwyth at 8 o'clock, arriving in Kington in time for the 4 pm train by which travellers can proceed to London, Bristol, and all parts of the south of England the same evening.'[3] In 1859 the retimed 4 pm from Kington, formerly the 4 30 with no connections, arrived at Hereford at 5pm to connect with the Gloucester and Paddington train which arrived in London at 11 pm and had only second class accommodation. With the disappearance of the stage coach the journey to Aberystwyth became more difficult rather than easier. In 1882 Thomas Skarratt, the Kington draper, wrote in his diary on his return from a holiday at Aberystwyth, 'After a tedious journey in which we had to change carriages three times, we arrived safe at home.'[4]

Endurance was a Victorian value, but the local traveller was not totally uncomplaining and in response to complaints about the accommodation for travellers at Leominster station it was announced in 1859 that a refreshment room had been erected there and leased to the licensee of the White Lion. At Kington, refreshment rooms were established just beyond the station precincts on a site near that now occupied by the roundabout. Both establishments were needed, for the Leominster and Kington railway soon acquired a reputation for unpunctuality, and unscheduled twenty minute waits at Pembridge whilst timber wagons were loaded and shunted caused protests at shareholders' meetings as did the inconvenience of the time-table for the long distance traveller.[5] In particular, before the opening of the Kington and Eardisley line, critics found the journey to Hereford, the county town, particularly tiresome, a 'painful process of waiting and shunting, shunting and waiting, taking up Mr Field's luggage in the shape of coal trucks, so that between this shunting and waiting on the line, and waiting at Leominster, a large portion of the day was occupied in reaching Hereford... a gig or a man's ten toes would accomplish the journey in as short a time.'[6]

Winter rail travel could still be particularly difficult and when in January 1881 'the Mail Cart for Hay and Glasbury failed to get further than Kingswood, the bags were brought back and put in the Eardisley train. This also got fast between Lyonshall and Almeley. Two of the carriages got off the rails; about three hours elapsed before it was extricated.'[7] Even so this misfortune was no more than a local difficulty in comparison with what happened to the Aberystwyth mail coach in January 1854:

'6th January: The weather still as severe. No intelligence as yet of the Mail Coach, guard, or horses, leaving Aberystwyth on the 3rd.

8th January: News arrived of the Mail being extricated from the snow on Radnor Forest after being buried since the previous Tuesday.'[8]

Kington was not slow in attempting to exploit all the commercial potential of its newly acquired position as a railhead. The emergence of Llandrindod Wells as a spa town encouraged the brief revival of a stage coach service with Kington in 1875. 'A well appointed four horse coach' was introduced which ran daily to Llandrindod Wells, Sundays excepted, taking three hours for the twenty-one mile journey and two and three quarter hours for the rather less uphill trip back. At week-ends it provided a connection with the 4.45pm London train and returned to Kington on Monday morning for the 11.10am. [9]

Rather optimistically, the railway was also seen as a means of developing Kington as a resort and tourist centre. When efforts were made in 1908 to popularise the town, advertisements were taken in railway guides and the possibility of having photographic views of the town placed in railway carriages of the GWR was discussed. The 1907 *Holiday Haunts* of the GWR, price one penny, contained a full page advertisement for Kington as, amongst other things, 'the finest residential neighbourhood in the west of England.' Its 'pure water and perfect sanitation'[10] and, excellent endowed grammar school, established in 1625,[11] and its indisputably bracing climate were offered as other attractions. There was also a half page paragraph of text about the attractions of Kington and the names and addresses of eleven landladies, three of whom offered stabling, and two others proximity to the urban district's recreation ground as special reasons for staying with them. There were, too, the first rumblings from what was to become the railway's most successful rival: motor tours to Llandrindod Wells and the Elan Valley were advertised.

In March 1910 the *Kington Times* was advertising the second edition of a *Guide to Kington: New Health Resort,* containing fourteen illustrations and available from Stevensons, 33 High Street, for 2d. a copy. Perhaps the attempt to project Kington as a resort met with some success, for in that same year the author of an article in the *Railway Magazine* could 'confidently recommend this district for a country holiday either for the railwayist, tourist, or antiquarian, for it teems with scenes of the most picturesque and romantic character......Through coaches from London run on the 10.50 am via Swindon and the 1.40 pm via Worcester and Hereford to Leominster. therefore necessitating only one change between London and Kington and New Radnor.'[12]

In August 1913 when Hanter Villa was offered for auction at the Oxford Arms, one of its selling points was its being only a quarter of a mile from Dolyhir station.[13] Likewise, Barton Farm at Kington was advertised in 1919 as being within half a mile of Kington Railway Station, GWR, and Great Quebb at Eardisley claimed the twofold attraction of being 'two and a half miles from Eardisley Station, Midland, and three and a half miles from

Kington Railway Station, GWR.' The Duke's Arms at Presteign, 'a Family and Commercial Hotel,' advertised its chief amenity as being the fact it was only 'three minutes from the Railway Station.'

At the station passengers were met by one of the horse-buses run by the local hotels and when the Burton Hotel acquired a new keeper in 1882 he was thought to be particularly enterprising because it was his intention to keep post horses and to run a bus to meet the trains. It was also now possible from 1860 to read the London papers in Kington on the day of their publication, thanks to Edward J Partidge's General Newspaper Agency's arrangements with the Leominster and Kington Railway Company, delivered free at any of its stations 'at an exceedingly low rate per annum, viz:

		If paid in advance
The Times (Carriage free)	£6 17 0	£6 10 0
Morning Star	1 17 6	1 12 6
The Standard	1 17 6	1 12 6
Daily Telegraph	1 17 6	1 12 6' [14]

The additional luxury of the electric telegraph, the wires and poles of which followed the railway line, came to Kington in 1870.[15]

The railway not only enlarged the horizons of local inhabitants, but also brought the outside world, at least on occasion, to Kington, as when in June 1878 the offer of a Shilling Day Excursion caused so many trains to be run from Birmingham and other places there was 'such an influx of visitors that Kington is not likely to have again very soon.'[16] There was such an influx, however, in August 1885 when there was a review of Army Volunteers at Kington. Admission was sixpence and was 'witnessed by several thousand people of all classes from Town and Country . . . Special trains brought many from Leominster, Presteign, and Radnor.'[17]

The railway made specialists and experts readily available. Thus Ewan Christian, architect to the Ecclesiastical Commissioners, was able to travel down from London by train to supervise the restoration of churches at Eardisley, Clifford, and Glascwm which, for all its present day remoteness, in 1891, when the rebuilding took place, had the choice of five railway stations within a radius of ten miles. Likewise, when New Radnor parish church had to undergo extensive repairs in 1878, the availability of the railway meant that the specialist Tewkesbury firm of Thomas Collins could be employed for the task and that their workmen could travel by train. The same firm was used in 1885 to rebuild Kinnerton church and once again the New Radnor railway proved useful.

Sometimes the trains carried rather more reluctant passengers. When the youngest son of the proprietor of one of Kington's shoeshops was brought before the magistrates for being disorderly and 'for wanting to fight the police on Fair Night' he was unable to pay the fine. He was given twenty-one days hard labour instead and 'handcuffs were put on him and he was marched off by two policemen to the Railway Station en route for Hereford Gaol.'[18] The railway also generated a certain amount of crime, the *Kington Times*, for example in January 1914, reporting 'An amazing series of burglaries' wherein the 'sweetmeat automatic machines' at Kington, Stanner, Dolyhir, and New Radnor had all been broken into on one night and the money they contained extracted. The building of the railways often offered employment to the local lawyers as when in 1875 James Meredith, the proprietor of Kington's Iron Foundry, claimed damages from the Kington and Eardisley Railway which had allegedly damaged the foundry's water supply. The case was heard by the Under Sheriff and a jury in the, no doubt, convivial atmosphere of the Oxford Arms. Dansey Green Price, son of the Company chairman, Sir Richard Green Price, appeared for the railway as did Edmund Cheese, another Kington lawyer, and Company Secretary. The jury found in favour of James Meredith and he was awarded £350 damages.[19]

The trains soon had an established role in the *rites de passage* of the local inhabitants. In 1880 a couple started a new fashion and were married early in the day 'so as to leave by the 11.15 train. The Band played at the Cross while their friends were discussing the Wedding Breakfast,'[20] and when the vicar of Kington died in 1888 'the corpse was conveyed to the Railway Station to be taken to Ashow, about two miles from Leamington. The Church Choir and a very large number followed the hearse and all the shops en route were closed.'[21] When Ernest Hopton, who was killed on the railway at Shrewsbury, was laid to rest in the graveyard of the Gore chapel, his coffin was brought back to Stanner 'by the train arriving shortly before 2 o'clock and a large number of sympathizers joined the train at Kington to attend the funeral and to show their heartfelt sympathy.'[22] Railway workers were respected members of the community and it was also reported that Mr Thorn the stationmaster of Stanner and Mr Tranter of Dolyhir station attended the funeral.

The clergy were quick to appreciate the usefulness of the railway. In April 1860 the Revd Henry Thomas Whateley, MA, was offered the benefice of Kington by his uncle the bishop of Worcester. Before accepting the living he travelled by train to Pembridge to consult the Revd James Davies at Moor Court, who was to let him know if he would be at home to receive him, 'sending word by the train that leaves Pembridge at 11.30 by Allen the Guard.'[23]

There was no Cottage Hospital at Kington until 1889 and until then the railway provided the town with an ambulance service. In June 1884 'Mr Banks' coachman was out on Hergest Ridge airing one of the horses. For some cause the bridle bit broke....., the man fell or was thrown off and broke his leg near the ankle. Fortunately, he was seen by someone shepherding and came to his help. He was conveyed in a trap to the Station thence per train to Hereford Infirmary.'[24]

Not all the passengers, however, carried by the railway were human. Lord Hill's Otter Hounds, for example, were accustomed to travel to the hunt by train to and from Titley. On December 21st 1880 Thomas Skarratt noted that 'the Dead Poultry Market for Xmas today was the largest I ever remember... The lot were cleared at satisfactory prices and a train sent from Birmingham specially to convey them to their destination.'[25] The drovers who used to drive their cattle and sheep through Kington to the Midland and London markets took advantage of the trains, and down to the very end of Kington's railway career the annual sheep sale was the busiest day of the year requiring additional staff and five or even six special trains to take the animals away. Along, with Marlborough and Craven Arms, Kington was one of the busiest stations in the country in the number of sheep it handled. It was said that between 8,000 and 9,000 head of cattle a year passed through the Kington goods yard. The opening of the Newtown and Llanidloes line in 1862 was in some measure a set-back for Kington, but it was still important for handling livestock. Some hoped that the arrival of the railway would facilitate the establishment of a horse fair at Kington to rival that of Huntington. Amongst these was Richard Parry, the Kington historian, who wrote in March 1856 to the editor of the *Hereford Journal*: 'Kington is now become a railway terminus, and it is in the opinion of many influential persons with whom I have conversed upon the subject, and amongst whom are several horse-dealers, that a good horsefair can be established in the town, as the railway affords an easy and cheap mode of transit for the horses and owners to any part of the kingdom.'[26] There were also those who hoped that the local line would acquire substantial mineral traffic. There were the local dreams of finding coal and in 1863 a shaft was sunk on Bradnor Hill in the hope of finding lead.

The success of the annual Presteign horse races was enhanced by the coming to that town of the railway: a local diarist recording 'the GWR arrangements being well-appreciated and bringing a considerable influx of visitors. Some of the horses arrived the evening before and the early train brought several more thus giving opportunity for an early morning gallop.'

The Kington branch of the Farmers' Union, however, at times expressed its dissatisfaction with the facilities of its local railway, complaining, for example, in February 1911 that cattle to be sold at Leominster market had to leave on the 6.30 am train for a sale only fourteen miles away which did not begin until 10.30 am. The protest was successful and the cattle train was retimed for a 7.20am departure.

The railways soon became the largest local source of employment. The stations at Kington, Presteign, New Radnor, and Eardisley all had their full time staff. At Kington in the 1950s, with closure at hand, there was the stationmaster, a booking clerk, a checker in the goods office, and porters. There was a passenger train guard for the mixed trains to and from Presteign, a shunter, two signal-men, and two engine drivers, two firemen, and a shedman. Along the line there were crossing-gate attendants. It also had its own branch of the National Union of Railwaymen, inaugurated in January 1914.

The railway brought its casualties. too. Some were accidental: a severe storm in 1874 caused the Back Brook at Kington to flood whilst the New Radnor extension was being built, and a small girl who attempted to cross the brook by a plank used by the workmen was knocked off by the wind and drowned.[27] A few years later, in May 1877, 'an old Welshman named Jones, got his small wagon loaded and started on his way back with two horses. Having got a short distance beyond the railway bridge at Flood Gates, the train from Radnor came by and frightened the horses and he, not being able to manage them, was knocked down. The wagon passed over him, breaking his arm and thigh, also injuring him internally.' He was taken home, near Llandegley, in the horse bus of the Oxford Arms, where he died soon after his arrival.[28] The stations themselves also claimed their victims, as when in December 1884 Mrs Charles Caldicott of Kington 'was knocked down by a Railway Train at Leominster Station and badly hurt, ribs broken and injury to the head.'[29] The ever-enterprising Edward Partridge of Leominster was not slow to draw the public's attention to the services of 'The Railway Passengers Assurance Company' of which he was the local agent.[30]

The local equine population was slow in adapting to the new method of locomotion. In 1911, when trains had been running to Almeley for over thirty-five years, the *Kington Times* reported that while driving a trap past Almeley station a nasty accident was sustained by a certain Mr Harris of Kymin Cottage. 'A slight rumbling from the station startled the horse which bolted down the road. Mr Morris was thrown from the vehicle and alighted heavily on the side of the road. The vehicle overturned, the shafts being broken.'[31]

Other mishaps were less accidental: in August 1888 'a sad occurrence took place on the Railway a little way behind the plank bridge leading up to the Barton Meadows. Old Harrison, head moulder in the Casting House at the Foundry, was strolling up the line. The 11.13 Train from Radnor ran over him and cut his head off all but two little strips, also part of one of his feet. Whether by accident or suicide is not known. An Inquest having been held, the Jury brought in a verdict of accidental death which enables his widow to receive £100 from an Insurance Company. But many persons are of the opinion it was his own doing. He was seen sitting on the side of the Line just before the Train came.'[32]

Serious accidents involving only the trains seem to have been rare but when they did occur they were given generous press coverage, as when the *Hereford Times* of March 14th 1914 reported:

'Railway Accident: Alarming Scene at Kington. The 9.10 train from Kington to Eardisley had just left Kington station but instead of going on the main line ran down a siding in which were standing three empty horse boxes against a stop block. The engine dashed into these, carrying them some distance and smashed the stop block. One of the horse boxes was turned completely over and rested on top of another. The horse boxes were smashed very badly, the iron work being twisted into extraordinary shapes. The impact threw the engine of the passenger train off the line and considerable damage was done to the permanent way. The fireman jumped off, but the driver stuck to the engine and luckily only sustained a shaking.......The line between Kington and Leominster was blocked by the wreckage until a breakdown gang arrived from Hereford and managed to get the line clear for trains to proceed past the accident by one o'clock.'[33]

It is perhaps significant that the train was carrying only one passenger, a Mr Lewis T Turner who was the Clerk to the New Radnor magistrates, and lived at Kinnerton Court. 'He was considerably bruised and shaken and was driven home later in the morning.' A few months earlier, apparently, another accident had occurred in this siding when a goods train ran away and dashed into the stop block, causing 'considerable damage to the rolling stock and the permanent way.' The *Kington Times* made no mention of the accident, though it covered a railway mishap in New South Wales which occurred at the same time. On the other hand, an enterprising local photographer was not slow to produce picture post cards of the accident.

There had been, however, occasional accidents in building the railway, as, for example, in 1879 when the GWR bought the old gas works which were near the station at Kington. These works had been replaced by new ones in 1873 and the railway company now proposed to extend the goods yard so that it would be easier to load timber trucks. Whilst the old gas works were being dismantled there was an accident in which when one of the workmen was in an old tank, there was an earthslip which knocked him down and broke his legs.[34]

Those who lived in Radnorshire and who voted Liberal saw the county's increased prosperity and trade as a blessing brought by the railway through the efforts of Sir Richard Green Price, the county's Liberal MP:

'But for the railway, much of the land in the county would be valueless, it had not formerly kept a goose to an acre. But now, look at it in all its verdure, and to whom were thanks due? By what means other than the railway could they have got their lime for the land? The railway had increased the value of their sheep and the general trade and commerce of the county and to Sir Richard Green Price this was mostly due.'[35]

Certainly the New Radnor railway played its part in the improved availability of agricultural lime. The Old Radnor Lime, Roadstone, and General Trading Company, with its offices in Kington, was founded in 1875, the same year as the New Radnor railway. Its chairman was Charles Chambers, the railway's contractor. Its manager was Charles Wellington Lloyd who was also secretary to the Kington Water Company, and its secretary was the local lawyer, Edmund Cheese, who was also Company Secretary to the Leominster and Kington Railway. Thus, a combination of enlightened self-interest and symbiosis brought about the foundation of Old Radnor Trading Company which by 1884 had fifty-six railway site depots in Radnorshire, Breconshire, Herefordshire, and Shropshire, and was advertising itself as 'the largest lime works and best quality lime in the Kingdom. Our Quarries and Works at Old Radnor were never in a better and more complete state than they are at present, enabling us to produce the finest and purest quality Lime ever placed in the market and our plant being extensive and perfect in every detail, we can undertake punctuality in the execution of orders as no other Lime Works can do.'[36]

For most local people the greatest benefit bestowed upon them by the railway was the better and cheaper supply of coal. In January 1854, when the Leominster and Kington Railway was still far from complete, Thomas Skarratt reported that 'Coal so scarce in Kington that many are obliged to do without. A poor consolation to keep out the cold.'[37] The argument, however, that the new local railways were reducing the cost of coal for the local inhabitants was disputed. Some argued that they were keeping its price unnecessarily high. At the opening of the Presteign line one speaker had maintained that 'the little line from Titley to Eardisley was one of the most important lines that could be made in this district because it opened up the South Wales coal fields and was the only means of bringing the coal here.'[38] An anonymous correspondent to the *Hereford Times* saw this as a complete delusion:

'The line named does not open up the South Wales coal fields neither does it give any benefit in the way of reduction through rates nor can it while the local railway companies blindly rush into the arms of the GWR Company. Had the Kington and Eardisley line been entrusted to the working of the Midland Railway Company we should have had Derbyshire, Leicestershire, and other coals at such a price as would have compelled the GWR to reduce the rates of carriage for Welsh coal, for it is a fact well known to anyone acquainted with the local coal supply that the house coal collieries of south Wales almost exclusively run on the Great Western system who of course convey the traffic over their own lines, hence the whole supply of coal for Kington and Presteign still comes via Leominster at the rates enforced for years before the Kington and Eardisley line was constructed. It was not sufficient for the directors of our local railways to construct their lines and then to hand them over to a railway company already enjoying a monopoly of the district without any stipulation as to the rates they may charge for the conveyance of the various descriptions of minerals. I will not insult their intelligence by the supposition that they are not unaware of the very unfair charges imposed by the GWR Company for the carriage of South Wales coal to Leominster and Kington as compared with Hereford. Yet the fact of their existence is a very fair inference of the case. If they were to devote their attention and influence to an equalisation of these charges, coal might be brought to Kington, Leominster, and Presteign at considerably less cost than at present. But no, it is quite sufficient to meet at the statutory meetings, learn that the GWR have paid the rent, pocket their dividends and salaries, and return home.'[39]

The price of coal was a major local issue. Admiral Sir Thomas Hastings, KCB, Vice-chairman of the Leominster and Kington Railway, having lived in the district for thirty years, 'had noticed how the sources from which the poor had been supplied with fuel had been annually decreasing. The enclosure of waste lands, the exhaustion of woods, and other causes, the poor had of late experienced increased difficulties in procuring fuel, and nowhere was this difficulty more felt than in Radnorshire. Thus on the ground alone of enabling the poor to procure fuel on more easy terms he felt it his imperative duty to support this railway. Moreover, were he the trustee of £500 or so to be expended for the benefit of the poor in the neighbourhood of Kington or Presteign, he would immediately invest it in shares in the Leominster and Kington Railway under the deep conviction that by so doing he should effectually place within their reach the means of obtaining coal at a price considerably below that at which it could be procured, and that he could thus secure to them greater advantages than could result from any other application of trust money.'[40]

Before the coming of the Tramway the average price of coal was from 42s to 45s a ton, and it had to be laid-in during the summer. At any other time of the year it could cost as much as 67s a ton, and it was the Tramway which had reduced the price to 30s a ton. In 1857, after the opening of the railway, it was 15s a ton. Before the opening of the railway at Leominster the coal bill of the Kington Board of Guardians had averaged £92 per annum, but it had now been reduced to £28 per annum. Those who promoted the Kington and Eardisley Railway argued, rather optimistically, that good quality household coal could be delivered to Kington, if the line were built, 'for 10 or 11s a ton from South Wales. Coal for lime burning would come equally cheaply and an inexhaustible market would be opened for local produce.'[41]

Sir Thomas Hastings, contributing to the debate as to whether a line from Kington to Leominster was of greater benefit than one to Hereford, argued that the latter would shorten the distance to the county town 'by four miles and the time taken by express trains by some eight or ten minutes. On the other hand, the line from Kington to Leominster, at the cost of eight or ten minutes, afforded all the advantages of a direct route to the metropolis, and offered for the county's corn, wool, hops, wood, and cider direct communication with the great northern manufacturing districts, and would enable farmers to compete with the importers of corn from the United States. The prospect of the railway being extended from Woofferton, via Kidderminster, into the great manufacturing areas of the Midlands also had great advantages for Kington and Leominster.'[42]

Kington was eventually served by a surfeit of railway lines to the financial detriment of them all. But Richard Banks in 1863 remembered in

Kington 'standing at the King's Head and seeing four coaches all changing horses at the same time. A gentleman was standing at the door, the late Sir Frankland Lewis, and he remarked to Mr Jones of the Star and Garter, 'how is it that all these coaches pay? and he, in reply, uttered one of the greatest truths possible, the more coaches, the more travelling. This railway is not in competition with any other railway, but it would conduce to the success of every other line into which it could possibly run.'[43]

In the event, however, the railway failed to revive either New Radnor or Presteign's flagging prosperity and Kington fared little better. In 1861, four years after the opening of the line from Leominster, the population of Kington was 2,178, but by 1901 it had declined to 1,944, 1,819 in 1911, and 1,688 in 1921. In 1863 the vicar of Kington expressed his conviction that the railway would tend to promote the success of the town: 'he did not look to it as a means for carrying people away from the town as much as a means of bringing them into it.'[44] But he was mistaken. The taste for travel developed by cheap day tickets also helped to establish depopulation as the on-going scourge of Radnorshire and the border. Its accessibility gave many the ambition to move away to more prosperous or attractive areas. No doubt when AW Gamage gave up his shop in Kington High Street and travelled to London and set up his famous store in High Holborn, he went by train. Moreover, the gentry could now have goods and furnishings sent down from London in a greater and more fashionable selection, and their dealings with local shopkeepers and tradesmen declined. Even Meredith's iron foundry, Kington's largest industrial undertaking and which had supplied some of the original tramway, barely survived the century. The brave expectation expressed anonymously in the *Hereford Times* in 1862 that the railway would restore the little town of Kington to its former prestige so that it would again be 'the eye of Radnorshire' was never fulfilled.

NOTES

1. HT 5.4.1862.
2. HT 4.6.1859.
3. HT 28.5.1859.
4. TCS p.103.
5. HT 12.3.1859.
6. HT 5.4.1862.
7. TCS p.47.
8. Ibid., p.5.
9. HT 11.9.1875.
10. The accuracy of this claim is disputable. 'A water company was first formed in 1886 and by 1889 some houses were connected with water mains. But the number of such houses was comparatively few, and even in 1892 it was calculated that

only one house in a hundred had a bath and a tap, and none with hot water laid on. Most people continued to rely on their wells or the public pumps......The great improvement came in 1918 when the Urban District Council took over the water supply.' Howse, W.H., *Kington, Herefordshire*, Kington, 1989, p.22. The town acquired its first sewage scheme in 1892.
11. In 1632, in fact.
12. Husband, op.cit., p.191.
13. KT 2. 8. 1913.
14. Partridge, op. cit.,p.68.
15. News about the battle of Trafalgar and Nelson's death on 21st October 1805 did not reach England until 6th November.
16. TCS p.47.
17. TCS p.123.
18. TCS p.64.
19. It was a case of history repeating itself. in October 1822 Thomas Meredith claimed compensation for damage to the water supply of his foundry, for which he was offered, and declined, six sovereigns.
20. TCS p.76.
21. TCS pp.138,9.
22. KT 28.11.08.
23. Banks Archive.
24. TCS p.115.
25. TCS pp.85,6.
26. FRRP p.44.
27. KT 5.11.1938.
28. TCS p.29.
29. TCS p.119.
30. Partridge, op.cit.,p.67.
31. KT 11.2.1911.
32. TCS p.141.
33. HT 14.3.1914.
34. TCS p.63.
35. HT 28.3.1874.
36. *Kington Gazette* 28.10.1884.
37. TCS p.5.
38. HT 18.9.1875.
39. Ibid.
40. HJ 20.2.1862.
41. HT 5.4.1862.
42. HJ 20.2.1856.
43. HT 14.3.1863.

CHAPTER SEVEN: THE END

Neither the Leominster and Kington Railway nor the Kington and Eardisley Railway had their own stock; both lines were run under lease. The earliest GWR locomotives were 0-6-0 saddle tanks, built at Swindon in the 1870s. These were replaced at the turn of the century by 0-4-2 and 2-4-0 tanks which in turn gave way to class 14XX and class 58XX 0-4-2 tanks. Designed by Collett for light branch work, some of which were fitted for push and pull working, they were introduced in 1932/33 and became known locally as the 'Kington coffee pots'. 'These 0-4-2s are capable-looking machines, but hardly so generously girthed as their saddle tank predecessors on the line.' So commented a traveller in 1939 who went on to note that some of the branch's workings were interlocked with those of the Leominster-Bromyard line which continued to Worcester and that the few trains that worked through from New Radnor to Worcester were hauled by tender locomotives, usually Dean 0-6-0s.[1] The normal allocation to the diminutive Kington shed was two engines, numbers 5815 and 5806 in 1939, with three sets of men and these performed all the branch workings except the weekday goods to and from Leominster. At first, the passenger stock consisted of three or four coach sets of six wheelers weighing about 45 tons. Clerestoried, un-corridored eight wheelers appeared in the late 1920s and in 1939 the Presteign and Eardisley branches shared a train consisting of 'a brand new composite non-corridor bogie coach and a goods brake-van. The latter carried several churns full of water, either to supplement the engine's tank supply or for servicing the stations.'[2]

National events made little impact upon the Kington railways, though in March 1912 the GWR announced in consequence of the coal strike, to which of course steam trains were very vulnerable, that all day returns and excursion rate tickets were cancelled and that a restricted train service would be introduced as well.[3] But once introduced restricted services were reluctantly abandoned, so that in October 1912, more than six months after the strike had been settled, Kington Urban District Council wrote to the GWR complaining about the rail connections between Kington, Birmingham, and London. The train from London, for example, arrived at Hereford three minutes after the Kington connection left, an inconvenience which had arisen from the recent coal strike, but the connections were not restored with the settlement of the strike.[4]

In his reply the Divisional Superintendent at Gloucester regretted the severance of the connection between the train leaving Birmingham at 6.20 pm and the one from Leominster for Kington at 8.40 pm, but experience had shown it was impossible to work the Birmingham train at anything like its booked time. The late starts thereby caused to the Kington train were not thought to be fair to the passengers arriving by the 8 pm mail from Hereford who had, apparently, to wait such a long time at Leominster, especially as they were much more numerous than those arriving from Birmingham. The Divisional Superintendent went on to argue that practically the same circumstances applied to the train due at Hereford at 8 3 pm. The transfer from that train to the 8 pm mail was very small. Anyhow, he pointed out, it was not true that passengers had to leave Birmingham at 2.30 pm to reach Kington the same evening. One could, instead, leave on the 4.23 pm or the 4.40 pm via Shrewsbury and connect with the 8.45 pm from Leominster. Thus he concluded his reply to the council: 'I much regret therefore our inability to meet your wishes,'[5] and Kington had to make do with a rail journey of 4¾ hours from Birmingham, seventy miles away, at the average speed of 15 miles per hour.

The outbreak of the Great War in 1914 saw little difference in things until 1916 when the Eardisley line was closed and its track taken up, allegedly to be relaid in France. It is said, however, that it never got there, the ship carrying it being sunk in the English Channel by a submarine. The *Kington Times*, perhaps for reasons of national security, was very reticent about the wartime activities of the local railways and no mention was made of closing the Eardisley line or of taking up its track. But in July 1933 some railway carriage dwellings at Eardisley were condemned as being unfit for human habitation by Kington Rural District Council and one wonders whether these were carriages abandoned at Eardisley when the track was removed and which were subsequently taken over by homeless squatters.[6]

In September 1919 there was a strike of railwaymen against the threatened reduction of their wages. Lloyd George allowed Auckland Geddes, president of the Board of Trade, to provoke the strike by his intransigence; then stepped in himself and settled it on the railwaymen's terms. This was a great stroke for the National Union of Railwaymen and for their accomplished leader J. H. Thomas, a GWR engine driver. The strike was short lived and on October 11th the *Kington Times* announced 'trains again steamed up branch lines which had been silent and deserted for nine days. A telegram that the strike had been settled was received at Kington 8 pm Sunday evening. The men returned to work at Kington station Monday morning. There was no untoward incident during the week the men went on strike and everything passed off quite orderly.'

The railwaymen got what they wanted and their wages showed a greater improvement on their pre-war level than in any other industry so that in 1920, assuming their wages stood at 100 in 1914, their real wages now stood at 117.[7] Local sympathy was somewhat limited and one anonymous correspondent wrote to the *Kington Times*. rather inaccurately, about 'the glorious defeat of the railwaymen,' and another, at great length:

'I think it is well that railwaymen should know what the public think of their unreasonable demands. As a mother who lost her boy in the fight for freedom I'm asked what have our sons died for? Are such traitors as these to be allowed to continue to receive the same money from a concern which it is now acknowledged is not renumerative? Are we who have lost our sons to be taxed to pay these traitors? Why not do for them as the army did with poor young fellows who had lost their nerve momentarily under appalling conditions and were shot at dawn. Such men as these who are seeking for money they are not entitled to, are not fit to live in Old England. Exile them to one of our islands until they become reasonable. I feel very distressed by the present unrest in the country and the way in which well-paid railway servants have treated the traders of the country. Where are the local men who remained at home under the umbrella? The boys sacrificed everything to protect the very men who are now heading us to bankruptcy.....

A Mother affected.'[8]

A Leominster councillor denounced the railwaymen as a privileged class of people who had abused their privilege and this provoked a letter from a local railwayman who pointed out they had not taken advantage of their position in the war to extract larger wages. Food speculators were the people to blame with their inflated prices and the pre-war £1 in the pocket had lost 8/6d in value.[9]

In October 1920 representations were made to the GWR by the Herefordshire County Council about re-laying the line between Titley Junction and Eardisley, the metals of which were taken up as part of the war effort in 1916. The line had not been profitable and the Company was not enthusiastic for its reinstatement, using the excuse that there was still a considerable backlog of maintenance work to be done elsewhere from the war. On the other hand there was now a new social need for the railway: a sanatorium was opening in Almeley at Nieuport, the house connected with the Foley family in the days of the Tramway, and patients and their visitors would want to travel by rail to this remote outpost of health care.[10] The GWR had already resisted three approaches from the Ministry of Transport with resolute sympathy. When the necessary materials were available, then the railway would indeed be reinstated as soon as possible. The Ministry, for its part, was not prepared to use pressure or compulsory powers.[11]

Representatives of the local farming community met a similar response from the Ministry of Agriculture and it was not until September 1922 that the Titley-Eardisley line reopened for goods traffic between Lyonshall and Almeley. Work on relaying the track between Almeley and Eardisley was still in progress and on the completion of this work the restoration of passenger services was promised. The reopening of the line for general traffic took place on Monday, December 11th 1922, the first passenger train being the 9.5 am, which returned from Eardisley at 9.57 am. The occasion was marked in Kington by an informal luncheon at the Burton Hotel attended by representatives of the GWR, County Councillors, and local traders. One of the guests was Mr Walter Chambers who had assisted his father in building the railway and as a young man had attended its original opening in 1875.

The reopened Kington-Eardisley line offered a passenger service of three trains in each direction a day, one of which was mixed, and to travel by it must have been a triumph of hope over experience. According to the branch regulations:

'a) Up mixed trains requiring to attach or detach traffic at Almeley or Lyonshall Stations, must first run to the platform, and after dealing with the passengers, the complete train must set back clear of the lay-by siding points. After the goods vehicles have been secured, the passenger coaches must be put in the siding on the Down Side of the Line, and the Goods shunting can then be proceeded with.

b) Down mixed trains having on wagons for Lyonshall and Almeley should, as far as possible, detch the wagons at those Stations leaving any shunting necessary to be done on the Up journey from Eardisley to Titley Junction.

c) Timber traffic loaded on Timber Wagons must not be attached on Mixed Trains over the Branch, but must be confined to trains conveying Freight Traffic only, specials being arranged with same as necessary, making up with other Freight Traffic if required.'[12]

Six wheeled vehicles were not to work over the branch, and passenger trains, if hauled by an 0-4-2 tank locomotive, were not to exceed a load of 44 wheels; an 0-6-0 tank locomotive could haul a load of 60 wheels. 0-4-2 and 0-6-0 tank locomotives were the only types of locomotives allowed on the branch, and 'when a heavy fall of snow falls on a Saturday night or Sunday and there is a likelihood of the line being blocked on Monday, the Stationmasters at Almeley, Lyonshall, Titley Junction, and Kington, must visit their respective stations and confer with each other by telephone between 5.30 pm and 6.00 pm, the telephonic communications with Kington being made through Titley Junction.'[13]

The restoration of the Kington and Eardisley line, modest as its service was, gave rise to the hope that the plans which were announced by the GWR in 1923, as its contribution towards the easing of the economic depression, for the extension of its network into Central Wales, would revive the old plans for the westward extension of the line from New Radnor. Meetings were held at Aberystwyth, 'which would undoubtedly benefit from another route,'[14] and New Radnor, welcoming the proposal, but other local towns were not slow in bringing forward their own alternative ideas. Presteign urged the route from Presteign to Llanbister Road, and Whitmore Green Price, one of Sir Richard Green Price's several sons, who chaired 'an enthusiastic meeting' at Presteign in September 1923, expressed his fear that the GWR itself did not know what it wanted to do and when he asked whether it was to link the English Midlands with the west coast of Wales he could get no clear answer. The Presteign proposal was for the line from Kidderminster to travel to Presteign by way of Tenbury-Woofferton-Aymestrey-Byton and Shobdon. From thence it would follow the Lugg valley via Whitton and Llangunllo to join the LNWR near Llanbister Road.[15]

Leominster, too, had its aspirations, and in September 1923 the borough council sent a deputation to Paddington to press the claims of an extension from Leominster into Central Wales. They were told, however, that nothing was going to be done before 1924 and that the recent grouping of the railway companies whereby 120 companies were reduced to four, was likely to have an important but unspecified effect upon the railways of Central Wales.[16] In the event the only development of local significance was the opening in 1929 of Forge Crossing station on the Presteign branch though in October 1928 the *Kington Times* announced that the GWR and LMS were making arrangements, 'some of which will affect this district and would result in saving operating costs, an increase in efficiency and speed of services, and consequently where possible lower rates.'[17] Details, however, of these arrangements and of their beneficial effects, if any, never appeared in that paper.

By the begining of 1930, only eight years after its re-opening, the closure of the Eardisley line had become a real possibility. In the year following its reopening in 1922, the receipts, £3,587, were the best the line ever achieved, but they were never repeated. In 1925 the receipts from all services offered by the line were £2,512 whereas the total expenditure was £4,808, thus only half of the cost of maintenance and wages came from traffic receipts, indeed, the revenue from parcels traffic amounted to only £215. In 1929 the revenue from the line amounted to £2,513 whereas the expenditure was almost exactly the same as it was in 1925. The consistent decline in traffic receipts between 1923 and 1929 had meant for the GWR a 36% drop in revenue.

Those who advocated the social function of the line pointed out the needs of the patients and their visitors at Almeley's Nieuport sanatorium as well as those of the thirty-eight small-holders on the Nieuport estate. The closure of the railway would inflict serious hardship on the small-holders who, since they were ex-servicemen, could claim the community owed them a debt of loyalty and gratitude which could be best expressed by keeping the railway open and increased local support to help it pay. The local farmers, of course, also complained and sought help from the headquarters of the National Farmers' Union.

In February 1930 it was proposed that a conference should be held at Kington to protest against the line's closure and a deputation sent to the GWR. The meeting was held in Kington at the Burton Hotel, though the County Council, who it was thought could have been more helpful, wanted the meeting to be held at Hereford. The GWR was represented by the Divisional Superintendent and the District Goods Manager, both from Gloucester, and the Divisional Engineer from Shrewsbury. The Rural and Urban District Councils were represented, so too were the National Farmers' Union and local commercial enterprises like the Old Radnor Trading Company, and local worthies like the Vicar also attended. Mr Guy Chambers, JP, of the Old Radnor Trading Company, and whose father and grandfather were so closely connected with building local railways, was chairman.

The meeting was warned by the GWR that the railway was a commercial proposition and would be closed if it could not be made to pay: 'we are up against road transport.' The County Council's land agent held out the prospect of jam tomorrow because the line ran through the most densely timbered part of the county and the Council itself had 150 acres of timber which would mature within the next ten years and would be removed from the area by rail. The Forestry Commission also had extensive woodlands in the area. There was, too, the problem of poor loading facilities both at Almeley and Lyonshall stations and the fact that the developing bus services were more convenient with their door-to-door time-tables. Mr Chambers disputed the accuracy of the GWR's figures because they did not include the traffic generated by the Old Radnor Trading Company from the Dolyhir quarries, from which Eardisley was 44 miles away via Hereford and only 13 miles away via Titley and this would affect the company's costs immensely, and the wear and tear caused by extra heavy road vehicles would be unwelcome to the county surveyor. The GWR should remember that the Kington-Eardisley line also fed the Brecon and Hereford line of the LMS.[18]

The Kington and Eardisley branch survived another ten years when once again the outbreak of war gave the GWR the justification it sought for closing it down. It was finally closed on 1st July 1940 and when reopening was obviously uneconomic, it was abandoned, its track taken up, and its buildings and land sold.

Six days after the outbreak of the Second World War on September 3rd 1939, Kington received its first official evacuees: 'A large number of children and mothers evacuated from the Merseyside district arrived at Kington Station on Friday and Saturday. After receiving emergency rations they were taken to homes quietly and expeditiously in cars and buses.'[19] The railway, of course, came into its own once again during the war and in 1940, for example, after the evacuation from Dunkirk, trains brought survivors to Leominster where ambulances took some of the men to Hergest Camp, a mile south-west of Kington, but the majority coming to Kington completed their journey by train and local people can recollect taking sheets and clothing to Kington station where they helped in the transfer of men to the camp.

Locally the main brunt of the war effort fell upon the farmers and in June 1941 they were given permission 'for the second successive year' to harvest the grass growing on the railway slopes contiguous to their fields. It was estimated that there were 70,000 acres of grass on the embankments of the British railway system. The Welsh borders were important sheep and cattle rearing areas and this dispensation offered a useful and free extra supply of winter fodder.

In 1944 the 107th General Hospital of the United States Army opened at Hergest and between August 18th and 21st that year 527 patients were admitted, most of whom travelled by train, and between September 19th and December 31st Kington station received eleven hospital trains, each carrying some 300 patients. These hospital trains had come from the Military Hospital at Netley near Southampton, and local level-crossing keepers had to be warned of their unscheduled arrival once Gloucester Control had informed controls at Kington and Leominster. Their drivers were assisted by local railwaymen once on the Kington branch and the station itself, which, of course, was not designed to accommodate such lengthy trains, had to be adapted for its new function. The railings had to be removed from the station to facilitate the loading of the ambulances, and on their return journey the locomotives ran tender first because there was no turntable at Kington. The running round facilities were also very limited: 'as the distance between the facing Points and the Up Home Signal is only 44 yards, no vehicles must be attached to Engines running round their Trains, unless the Special authority of the person in charge is obtained, and before giving such permission, he must take Special steps to see there is no risk of the Engine fouling any Engine or Train coming from the Loco Shed or the direction of New Radnor.'[20] Another problem was that the rolling stock of the hospital trains was fitted with Westinghouse brakes whereas the GWR stock was exclusively vacuum braked. Consequently the trains were double headed, with a GWR pilot, and usually an LNER locomotive, with a Westinghouse braking system, hauling the carriages. Black-out regulations necessitated the use of a portable generator to light the platform when the trains were being unloaded at night.[21]

At Eardisley an American petrol, oil, and lubrication depot was established just outside the station by the junction with the Kington line, which was, however, defunct from July 1940. Consequently, an extra track was laid down, leading into what are now the saw mills. At the end of the war the removal of the surplus petrol and oil entailed, according to local memory, the services of at least nine trains of oil wagons.[22] Actual enemy action was virtually unknown in the Kington area though once, it is recalled, services were temporarily interrupted on the New Radnor line by a bomb dropped on Smatcher Hill.

The successful conclusion of the Second World War, in which they had played their modest part, did not, however, bring with it any revival in the fortunes of the Kington railways. The railways were nationalised in 1947, an event which passed unnoticed in the local press, though it caused the GWR lines to become part of the Western Region and the LMS at Eardisley to enter the Midland Region of British Railways. However, eight years later GWR tickets were still being used on the line. The most noticeable effect of the nationalisation was a decline in the personal nature of the relationships between staff and management. Thus the printed GWR regulations for the procedures to be followed in snowstorms in describing the duties of gangers on the Kington lines mentions them by name:

> 'Ganger Powell at Dolyhir to proceed to Dolyhir Station.
> Ganger Duggan at Marston Crossing to communicate with Pembridge Station.
> Ganger Abberley at Brook Bridge Crossing to proceed to Kingsland.'

The equivalent British Railways (Western Region) regulations for 1948 read:

> 'Ganger at Dolyhir to proceed to Dolyhir Station.
> Ganger at Kington to communicate with Kington.
> Ganger at Pembridge to communicate with Pembridge Station.
> Ganger at Brook Bridge Crossing to proceed to Titley.
> Ganger at Presteign Branch to communicate with Titley.'

The economic crisis of 1951 caused the Government to issue a directive to the nation to save coal. Consequently, the Railway Executive suspended the Leominster-Kington-New Radnor-Presteign services. The withdrawal of these local services was accepted with resignation, the chairman of Kington Urban District Council managing to say nothing stronger than that it was 'a very sad affair.'

From Monday, February 5th 1951, the year of the morale-boosting Festival of Britain, passenger services on the Kington railways were suspended until further notice and perishable goods normally carried by passenger train were now to be delivered from Leominster by lorry. It was all discussed rather lethargically by the Urban District Council: the chairman noting, recollecting no doubt the outcome of 'the temporary suspension' of the Kington and Eardisley service in 1940, 'there is always the danger of temporary suspensions becoming permanencies.' Another councillor thought that an urban district of 2,000 ought to have 'a morning and evening train, otherwise we will be off the map altogether... We have lost the gas works, road haulage, now the trains: it's the thin edge of de-urbanization.'[23]

It is an ill wind, though, that blows no one any good, and Primrose Motors of Leominster seized the opportunity and asked the Urban District Council to support its application to extend its bus time-table to Kington. It readily agreed, considering that 'Mr Bengry (its owner) is certainly doing more for us than the Coal Board are doing.'[24] The Kington Chamber of Trade, however, was rather more militant and sent yet another letter of protest to the authorities. It is noteworthy that in this final stage of Kington's railway history that the Chamber of Trade was consistently more active in attempting to keep the railway open than the Urban District Council which accepted events with stoic resignation accompanied by occasional mild ritual protest. There was, of course, an irony in the immediate cause of the closure of the Kington railways being a shortage of coal, for it was to bring coal more cheaply to the area that the local railway system was originally initiated.

On March 31st 1951, two months after its imposition, the *Kington Times* reported that the suspension of the passenger service between Leominster and Kington had been lifted, but not that between Titley-Presteign and Kington-New Radnor. Nine months later the ever vigilant Kington Chamber of Trade was addressed on the subject of the threat of closing the Leominster-Kington line by Mr Frank Seymour, the Kington stationmaster. He informed the meeting that the Railway Executive was considering the closure of the line to passenger traffic. In an attempt to boost passenger traffic cheap day returns were being issued from Kington on Wednesdays and Saturdays to Hereford, and were available four days a week to Leominster, but the public response had been poor. Mr Seymour urged the shopkeepers in his audience to use the railways to convey their goods and everyone in the town to make a greater use of the railway for excursions and party travel. For its part, the Chamber of Trade wanted daily cheap fares to Leominster and Hereford and the urban district council to replace the railway notice board which once adorned the wall of the Market Hall, so that the new cheap day tickets could be advertised in the very centre of the town.[25]

But it was all to no avail; further economies were made so that, for example, the level-crossings at Dolyhir, Stanner, Floodgates, and at Forge Crossing no longer had level-crossing keepers to open and shut the gates. Instead they were attended by the guard of the train and their keys were kept in a bunch at Kington signal box when not in use. 'Enginemen must approach crossings with caution and stop before and after passing each crossing to enable the guard to open and close gates.'[26] Another economy was the closure of the halt at Forge Crossing and of New Radnor station in 1952, the Kington and New Radnor branch being officially renamed the Kington and Dolyhir branch. The regulations were also modified for propelling a goods brake-van from Kington so that:

'When there is no traffic for Dolyhir up to three wagons and brake-van may be propelled from Kington to Stanner in daylight and clear weather. The brake-van must be the leading vehicle and the Guard must keep a sharp lookout. Speed during the propelling movement must not exceed 10 mph.'[27]

But the railway lingered on for another three years and then on January 7th 1955 the *Kington Times* announced that the Leominster-Kington branch line passenger service was to end within a month. The Rural District Council decided not to oppose the British Transport Commission's decision, it being the latter's argument that the numbers using the passenger service had decreased since 1954 and that on purely economic grounds the withdrawal of the service was justified because it would save £15,000 a year. Thus there was no alternative to closure. The Rural District Council tended to agree: one councillor had seen many times at Pembridge the train go by with only one passenger, and that a railwayman, and it was generally accepted by the councillors that closure was inevitable. 'Times have changed: I can remember when special trains had to be run to Eardisley to carry the many passengers, another councillor recollected, now there is nobody in the ordinary trains. No businessman would run a business to lose money, so why ask these people to? They are our railways and I object as much as anyone to their losing money.' There was, however, an extraordinary meeting called of the Kington Chamber of Trade to discuss ways and means of overturning the British Transport Commission's decision.

The local MPs were rather more positive than either the Urban District Council or the Chamber of Trade and in a bid to save the railway passenger service an appeal was made to the British Transport Commission by Alderman Tudor Watkins of Brecon and Radnor and Archer Baldwin of North Herefordshire to defer the closure of the line by a month until February 7th, some three weeks after the Leominster conference, they and representatives of the interested county and town councils arranged to discuss the problems of local transport on January 20th.

There were the usual complaints about the poor and inconvenient passenger service, but overstaffing was mentioned, too: a total of 13 men were apparently employed at Titley, Pembridge, and Kingsland stations, which must have been uneconomic. What Kington needed, it was felt, was a champion like Lord Rennell of Rodd, 'a personal friend of Sir Brian Robertson, who had taken up the matter for Presteign.' In the outcome, of course, friends in high places did no more for Presteign than not having them did for Kington. Another speaker felt that a diesel bus service on rails was what was wanted. There was also the widespread fear that closure would hasten the drift from the land. Surprisingly, at least in retrospect, was the assertion that 30,000 parcels a year went by the Kington and Leominster service.[28]

The British Transport Commission, however, had let it be known before the Leominster conference that it was against further discussion about local closures and declined to meet the deputation appointed at the conference. Thus on February 5th 1955 the last Leominster-Kington passenger train left Leominster station at 9.05 pm. Usually empty, it carried more than seventy passengers. There were no flags and no town band and the driver was Mr E Chapman of Leominster who had 39 years of railway service behind him, mainly on the Leominster-Bromyard line. The fireman was Mr J Davies who had been in service with the GWR since 1928, and the guard was Mr A Reynolds who joined the GWR in 1940. Leominster's station foreman, Mr F Caslyn, ceremonially shook hands with the driver before the train left for Kington where a black flag hung at the station entrance. Not surprisingly, the Kington stationmaster had never known so many tickets to be sold in one day, in fact it was four times the normal number. Some of these tickets from intermediate stations still bore the legend *Great Western Railway*. The final return journey was begun ten minutes after the train's arrival at Kington, and Mr Seymour, the stationmaster who had foretold this event to the Chamber of Trade in March 1951, shook hands with the driver and the passenger history of Kington's railways was over. This final journey back to Leominster was made to the inevitable accompaniment of exploding detonators on the line, and whistles from the engine. The day's events were appropriately completed by a collection at Leominster for the engine driver. Predictably, the Kington Chamber of Trade vowed to continue the fight for the line's restoration, though even their optimism did not now see this as necessarily being in its old form. The Urban District Council also paid its tribute though it had done little to prevent the service's demise.[29]

In February 1955 there was a Parliamentary debate on the subject of rural railway services and Mr Baldwin, MP for North Herefordshire, spoke during the second reading of the Transport Borrowing Powers Bill, doubting the British Transport Commission's figure of £15,000 for the line's losses. What was needed, he argued, was a fresh spirit in management: the Post Office did not close down village post offices or telephone boxes when they did not pay. Instead, they were kept open for public need and convenience. Moreover, the light industry which the town sought for its economic growth would never be attracted to Kington if it had no railway service.[30]

The rumblings of protest continued, largely orchestrated by the Chamber of Trade which still wanted the passenger service to Kington restored and told both the Transport Users' Consultative Committee and the British Transport Commission so.[31] It also outlined to the West Midlands Traffic Commission what it considered to be the serious position of railway and road services serving Kington and sought its assistance. Unfortunately for Kington and district the closure of the railway was seen as a national economic issue by the Transport Users' Consultative Committee who consequently would offer no further help. At the same time the isolation of the town and the surrounding district was aggravated by the announcement that bus services were also being curtailed between Kington-Hereford, and Kington-Brilley.[32]

There was a requiem, conducted by the Stephenson Locomotive Society, for the Kington railways on July 27th 1957 when a GWR 0-4-2T No 1455 hauled two coaches along the Kington branch as far as Dolyhir to celebrate the centenary of its opening. It could go no further west because the track of the line which had been kept open for freight the beyond Dolyhir to New Radnor had been removed. In January 1958 Kington Rural District Council was informed by letter that the Kington-Dolyhir branch, now only used for freight, was to close. A total of 255 tons of freight was dealt with in 1956 by the line, but by closing it £2,334 a year would be saved. Traffic had continued to decline but maintenance costs still increased, necessitating the total closure of the line, though deliveries and collections would continue at Kington station. 'There is nothing we can do about it' was the Chairman of the Rural District Council's comment, and the only one made at the meeting which received the news.

Mr Ernest Gregory, 1960-64, was the last stationmaster of Kington[33] and it was in his time that the Leominster-Dolyhir and Presteign sections of the line, over which for the last few years nothing more than a daily goods train had run, finally closed to goods traffic. The last train was hauled by the 0-4-2T No 1420 which like Mr Gregory's cap went into preservation and can nowadays be seen on the Buckfast Steam Railway. This last train ran on September 24th 1964, the same year in which Eardisley station, which up to then still served the Hereford-Brecon line, also closed.[34]

Little time was lost in taking up the now disused track and the station at Kington was demolished, but other railway buildings have survived. The crossing keeper's cottage and station house at Kingsland are now private residences[35] as are Eardisley, Lyonshall, Pembridge, and Titley stations. At Titley the awning and two platforms have survived. The crossing keeper's cottage at Marston Halt where the station consisted of a single wooden platform and where the guard of the last train of the day extinguished the oil lamps, was demolished in 1991, having been badly damaged by fire, but another keeper's cottage has survived at Forge Crossing. Kington's original 1857 station survives on the town's industrial estate, again as a private house, and carries a plaque commemorating its 1855-75 role. Nearby, a goods shed is now in industrial use and a shunter's hut languishes into dereliction. New Radnor station is now at the centre of a caravan park. Stanner station is now a Powys County Council store-house, and its neighbour at Dolyhir is the electrician's workshop for the Dolyhir and Strinds quarries of Nash Rocks. The station at Almeley has survived largely intact and is in agricultural use whilst that at Presteign has been demolished. In 1991 Eardisley station was dismantled and removed, lock stock and barrel, to Welshpool to be re-erected as the terminus building for the Welshpool and Llanfair Light Railway. Eardisley's large goods shed is now a private house. The track bed at Kington, Stanner, and Presteign has been re-used in parts in road improvement schemes.

The accepted local tradition is that the Kington railways were axed by Dr Beeching, a victim of a bad press if ever there was. The Transport Act of 1962 abolished the British Transport Commission and set up a new British Railways Board which was responsible for both the finance and the management of the railways. Dr Richard Beeching was appointed as chairman of the new board and his first task was to identify loss-making lines and, if needs be, to close them. He did this in two reports: *The Reshaping of British Railways*, 1963, and *The Development of the Major Railway Trunk Routes*, 1965. Since passenger traffic ceased to be carried on the Kington railways ten years before the publication of the latter report and it was only a skeleton freight service which was withdrawn in 1964, it would seem that Dr Beeching had no part in the shaping of the history of the Kington railways.[36]

NOTES

1. Hewitt, J D,'The Kington Branch of the GWR', *Railway Magazine*, September 1939, p.194.
2. Ibid. The water was to service the stations without mains water supplies.
3. KT 16.3.1912.
4. KT 12.10.1912.
5. KT 16.11.1912.
6. KT 22. 7. 1933.
7. A J P Taylor, *English History, 1914-1945*, Oxford, 1965, p. 141.
8. KT 4.10.1919.

9. KT 12.10.1919.
10. KT 19.10.1920.
11. KT 24.12.1920.
12. GWR notice No 2815, 11.12.1922. Mixed trains also ran between Kington and Presteign for which no train was to exceed 10 vehicles, including passenger carriages. Timber trucks were not to be attached to these trains though furniture vans could be.
13. Ibid.
14. Husband, J F,op.cit.,p.190.
15. KT 8.9.1923.
16. The basis of this speculation was probably that the Cambrian Railways by their incorporation into the Great Western and the incorporation of the London and North Western Railway and the Midland Railway, which locally met the GWR at Eardisley, into the newly formed London Midland and Scottish Company would facilitate some rationalisation of railway services in Central Wales.
17. KT 27.10.1928.
18. KT 15.2.1930.
19. KT 9.9.1939.
20. GWR Regulations.
21. Higginbotham, J, *Kington Camp*, Kington, 1980, p.79.
22. Ibid.,p.83.
23. KT 10.2.51.
24. Ibid.
25. KT 12.1.52.
26. BR Western Operating Area Regulations 1952.
27. Ibid.
28. KT 14.1.1955.
29. KT 11.2.1955.
30. KT 18.2.1955.
31. KT 6.5.1955.
32. KT 24.6.1955.
33. His stationmaster's cap is an exhibit in Kington Museum which has several memorials of Kington's railway history.
34. It was part of the 'Hereford Concentration Scheme' and there was some redeployment of staff in consequence. The two delivery lorry drivers stationed at Kington were moved to Hereford; a Kington signalman was moved to Leominster as a signal lampman; an Eardisley signalman/temporary goods porter and a Presteign leading porter became leading porters at Hereford; two goods porters from Kington and a checker from Eardisley became goods porters at Hereford; the head shunter at Titley took early retirement; and a leading porter from the station at Pembridge and a leading goods porter from the station at Kingsland left the railways. The services of a temporary goods porter at Eardisley who had been unsuccessful in his applications for other posts, 'should be dispensed with.......All staff concerned should be informed that a number of posts affording promotion to staff locally will be advertised in (the) next vacancy list. This could result in certain staff being promoted to posts other than as allocated above, also create vacant posts for others.' British Railways (Western Region) circular from the Divisional Manager's Office, Cardiff.

35. Mr Ernest Savory, the stationmaster at Kingsland from 1946-1959 bought the stationmaster's house and still (1991) lives in it. He joined the GWR in 1927 at the Hereford Goods Depot. In 1932 he was promoted to Ross on Wye where he was a booking and goods clerk. In 1935 he moved on to Grange Court near Gloucester until he was called up for military service in 1940. He returned to the GWR in 1946 and when he was made redundant in 1959 he moved on to Tenbury where he remained until redundancy again overtook him in 1964.

36. It might be appropriate at this stage to mention another, much more innocent, local tradition which is equally ill-founded. It is related that one Saturday afternoon that Dolyhir United were playing football against a visiting team on their lineside pitch. The ball landed in a truck of a passing goods train en route to New Radnor and the match was abandoned until the train returned and the ball was retrieved. There were, however, no Saturday afternoon goods trains between Kington and New Radnor and had there been both drivers and fireman would have noticed the game with interest and would have stopped the train to retrieve the ball. Another legend is that during the Second World War when Americans were stationed at Kington, early one evening some of them called at the Tavern for a quick drink. They were not off-duty and did not stay long, but to avoid the US military police they drove their jeep on to the railway line at Kington station and drove along the track to Titley Junction where they returned to the road and motored to the Holly Bush on the outskirts of Lyonshall where they spent the rest of the evening, uninterrupted by the authorities. (Higginbotham, op. cit., p.81). Finally, one wonders how the trains ever reached their destinations or, indeed, ran at all if one is to believe all the idyllic accounts handed on to the authors of ticketless passengers getting on and off at will at the trackside, the number of meals of fried eggs and bacon cooked on the fireman's shovel, the hundredweights of mushrooms picked en route, whilst passengers patiently looked on, and the number of children who rode on the footplate between Dolyhir and New Radnor.

CHAPTER EIGHT: EXCURSIONS, EXPLANATIONS, AND PERSONALITIES

T he railway continued to offer cheap day and weekend excursions to the end of its local history. In 1910 a two-day excursion to London by rail cost 8/6d.[1] In 1932 the LMS offered an express Sunday excursion to see the Blackpool illuminations, leaving Leominster at 10.55 am and Blackpool for the return journey at 9.30 pm, the return fare being 7/6d.[2] In competition the GWR offered a weekday excursion to London, leaving at 7 am, for which the return fare was 14/-.[3] At a more local level the *Kington Times* announced that 'Kington football enthusiasts should note the fact that a half-day excursion will be run to Presteign for the Otway Cup Final. The train will leave Kington. Return fare 1/-[4] In 1933 the cheap trip from Kington to London for the Manchester City v. Everton Cup Final cost 14/-. At the same period, day returns to Hereford were available every Saturday from Kington, the third class return fare being 2/- and the special cheap rates offered every year 'from all parts for the Kington Show' were widely used.

Sometimes the two companies seem not to have done their market research very carefully as when in February 1933 the GWR advertised its excursion rate fares to the British Industries Fair in London and Birmingham 'which should be visited by all business men.'[5] Kington was a town of small-scale traders rather than substantial business men. In 1933 summer tickets were available at 1d a mile and one could visit the Isle of Man TT races for 16/6d. An innovation in July that year was the 14/3d GWR outing by rail and Thames steamer to Windsor, leaving New Radnor at 6.40 am.

The most successful railway outings, however, were the Sunday School excursions and it might not be too fanciful to see a connection between the decline of the local railways and of attendance at the local churches. As early as April 1913 the *Kington Times* announced that the Leominster Wesleyan Sunday School had made arrangements with the GWR to run an express excursion to Weston super Mare, offering 'a vista of pleasure, a visit to winsome Weston.' The train was to leave Leominster at 5.40 am and to set out from Weston for the return journey at 8.45 pm. The actual event took place on May 17th 1913 when 'a finely equipped corridor train consisting of thirteen coaches conveying 400 passengers left Leominster promptly and arrived at Weston fifteen minutes early.' But not everything went as planned and some unspecified 'inconvenience to passengers' occurred between Bristol and Weston for which, again unspecified, steps were to be taken by the committee on future occasions to prevent its recurrence. The trippers arrived back at Leominster at 2 am the next morning.

The destinations of some of these excursions seem strange to modern travellers, as when in May 1930 a railway excursion was arranged from Leominster to Port Sunlight and the world's largest soap factory. The travellers were, apparently, 'deeply impressed by the wonders of the factory, discovering that labour at Port Sunlight wears a smiling face.'

The first church outing by rail from Kington seems to have been in August 1933. Arranged by 'the very popular and energetic vicar of Kington, the Revd RDR Greene, CF', the parishioners went to Rhyl on what was described by the *Kington Times* as 'a tremendous train... consisting of eleven large modern corridor coaches. Upholstered with every eye to comfort. Five at least of these will be for the Kington party which will be numbered about 300, with another available if needed, with two for the Titley party and two for the Lyonshall party. The Lyonshall party will be brought through to Kington and attached in front of the train and on return will be promptly returned from Kington to Lyonshall by a waiting engine to ensure a quick and comfortable journey home.' The return fare to Rhyl from Kington was 7s for adults and 3/6 for juveniles.[6]

But the popularity of these parish trips was short-lived and two years later, in 1935, when the vicar arranged another trip, this time to London, only 200 people from Kington and district availed themselves of the facility of a special train. They left at 10.15 am and arrived back in Kington at 2 am the next morning.[7] The Festival of Britain in 1951 saw a modest revival of the day excursion and British Railways six months before the Festival opened was inviting local clubs and organisations to plan their excursions by rail to the festival or to use the special train which was to serve the Leominster and Kington district in July 1951 with accommodation for 500 passengers.[8]

The swan-song of the large scale special Sunday School rail excursion as far as Kington was concerned occurred in July 1954 with a train to Barry Island. The train itself was seen by the local paper as the wonder of the age and perhaps British Railways made a conscious effort to offer their Kington patrons the best and thereby to secure future traffic:

'The long train of ten of British Railways, modern vestibule coaches including a restaurant car arrived at Kington Station on Wednesday evening. It attracted considerable local interest and several parties were shown over the train by the station staff. All were astonished at the improvements incorporated in the new vehicles, the extensive window space and the comfort of the seats attracting special attention and remarks were heard that the first class seats were equal to the best easies at home. The guard's brake compartment, compactly fitted with all train working devices and accident, fire-fighting, and ambulance equipment and a comfortable swivel seat for the guard, attracted attention. The train was divided on Thursday morning and five coaches sent to Presteign for the Presteign Church Sunday School and the Methodist Sunday School parties and Mr Crawfurd's party, all numbering over 200, to join up with the Kington portion which included New Radnor Church and Chapel Sunday School parties, Old Radnor Sunday School, and many passengers from Kington. There were over 400 on the train when it left and an enjoyable day was spent at Barry. An excursion to Porthcawl has been provisionally arranged for August 24th.'[9]

But the revival of interest in travelling by rail was ephemeral and there was no mention in the columns of the *Kington Times* of the Porthcawl trip having materialised.

The closure of the Kington railways was the inevitable consequence of the rise of motor transport; poor local service; and a detachment, either deliberate or unconscious, on the part of the GWR from the needs of the local communities it served.

The rise of both the public and private motor vehicle presented the local railways with a challenge they could not meet. As early as October 1919 announcements appeared in the press about 'a proposed motor omnibus service for Herefordshire' by the Birmingham and Midland Motor Omnibus Company for permission to run over various routes in the district. The County Council supported the application despite murmurings about the county's roads not being strong enough for such traffic and that their reconstruction and repair would cost hundreds of thousands of pounds.[10] It seems that Kington was first served by a bus service in December 1919 when AM Bird of Wigmore began regular market-day services, including one to Kington.[11] In the following June, Kington acquired its first resident bus proprietor in the person of Mr WA Owens who started business with a 14/16 seater charabanc converted from a war-time ambulance with which he offered the town a weekly service to Aberystwyth.[12] Three years later, in 1923, Kington acquired a direct road link with Hereford when Yeomans provided one return journey a week on Sundays[13] and then, in November 1924, Crossville, the expanding North Wales company, linked Kington and

Llandrindod Wells.[14] Towards the end of the period 1916-1922, when the Kington and Eardisley branch was closed, 'Darling's Blue Bus' emerged at Eardisley and its services were particularly appreciated by the children who had previously travelled to school by train.[15] Mr R O Darling lived at Eardisley and in 1928 the needs of Kington were served by another local citizen, Mr C T Sargeant, who developed a small network around the town of market day services which, though much changed in form, still exist today. Yeomans of Canon Pyon introduced their Hereford and Kington service c.1930 and this, too, still exists.[17]

For the summer months of 1929 the 'Original Coach Service' ran between the Black Swan at Leominster which it left on Mondays, Wednesdays, and Fridays at 9.45 am, for Aberystwyth. It called en route at the Talbot, Kington, at 10.30 am, and could offer its passengers 'accommodation for suitcases.' In August 1933 Yeomans Motors offered a day return to the Shrewsbury Floral Fete, coaches, as they were called, leaving the Market Hall, Kington, at 9 am. The fare was 5/6d and passengers were also picked up at Wootton, Almeley, Lyonshall, and Brilley.[18] That same year Burnham's Grey Luxury Coaches Express Service achieved what the Kington railways had long and unsuccessfully tried to offer, a through service to Aberystwyth, described by the company as 'the Biarritz of Wales', departing for Cardigan Bay from Leominster at 9.25 am and from Kington forty-five minutes later.[19] The summer of 1934 saw the Black and White Bus Company advertising in the *Kington Times* its 'improved Motor Coach services from Leominster to Kington, Hereford to Kington and both on to Aberystwyth, and to Oxford and Cheltenham in the other direction.

By October 1937 Primrose Motors of Leominster had a well-established and equally well-advertised daily service, including Sundays, between Leominster and Kington, which easily outstripped what was on offer from the GWR.[20] The following year saw Yeomans offering a special day trip to Birmingham 'in luxury coaches equipped with heaters', leaving Kington at 9.10 am for 6/- return.[21] The Second World War gave the railways something of a respite but competition was soon renewed afterwards and in 1951, the year of the Festival of Britain, with a languishing railway service, Presteign Urban District Council supported Yeoman's application to the Traffic Commissioners for a bus service between Presteign and Kington.[22]

Country bus companies could offer comfort and initiative far beyond the resources of a country branch line: for example, an Easter Sunday evening mystery tour leaving Lyonshall at 5.45; Kington 6.15; and New Radnor 6.30, for which the fare was 2/6d. A mystery trip by rail was an impossibility from Kington with dead ends at New Radnor and Presteign and with Eardisley and Leominster as the only alternatives. But for the bus traveller there was a half-crown return evening trip to Hereford and on Easter Monday a special bus for those who wanted to see Hay play Kington in the Challenge Cup or the Hereford steeplechasing. The invitation was 'to ride to music in Radio luxury coaches, equipped with heaters.'[23] The alternative by rail was six wheeled non-corridor compartmented coaches. The bus companies could offer greater variety with only one vehicle to fill rather than a whole train, so that in June 1935 Yeomans were able to offer excursions to Barry Island, Aberystwyth, and the Aldershot Tattoo, Three Counties Show, and, perhaps most popular of all, the Lyonshall dance. That same month the Kington Women's Unionist Association went to Porthcawl for their annual outing in two motor coaches. The weather, we are told, was ideal.

The motor car, too, soon became a formidable rival to the railway. James Fryer of Leominster was regularly advertising in the *Kington Times* in the early 1930s four different models of Austin car, from the Austin Seven upwards, all under £200. In April 1931 his advertisement began to ask: 'Are you a member of a two car family?' If not, then it was time to realise that 'all the world loves the Rover Family Ten' which for only £189 could put you into the two car category. James Fryer also had weekly advertisements for Morris and Wolsey cars, from £110 for the two-seater Morris Minor to £395 for the Morris 25 saloon: 'Morris, the car you are proud to own. The outstanding attractions of a 1934 Morris range from syncromesh all-speed gear box, automatic clutch and free wheel, Lockheed hydraulic brakes, cruciform frames, equipoise engine mountings, automatic ignition control, hydraulic shock absorbers, direction indicators, and real leather upholstery'.[24] The GWR accepted the arrival and challenge of the car and reacted positively. From February 1934 its weekly advertisement in the local paper carried the addition: 'Park your car at any GW station.' Herefordshire's roads, of course, were ill-suited to any dramatic rise in road traffic and in October 1950 Presteign WI passed a resolution 'that a 20 mph speed limit be imposed on roads through villages which should be rigorously enforced.'

Cars carried their passengers from door to door and buses started and finished in the town or village centre. This was not the case with the railways. Even the station at Kington was on the very edge of the town; those at New Radnor and Almeley were three quarters of a mile from the communities which bore their name; Kingsland and Pembridge stations were a mile from their villages and Titley Junction was nearer to two miles from Titley itself. Only Lyonshall station was near the centre of its village.

The emergence of the car was accompanied by that of the lorry and van and in July 1927 Fryers announced: "They are coming," the whole Chevrolet commercial vehicle range will arrive here on Tuesday, July 5th.' In 1875 the Old Radnor Trading Company had 26 depots in various local railway stations, but the arrival of motor transport had reduced these to eight by 1939. Likewise, at one stage the company had 240 private trucks transporting lime, stone, and coal, but by the time the railways were nationalised in 1947 this number had fallen to eighty. The GWR itself acquired its own lorries, and two were stationed at Kington displacing the draymen and their horses and carts which had previously done their duties.[25]

Finally, mention should be made of the humble bicycle as a rival to the railway. In February 1962 a railway man, Mr F G Thomas, of Kington, retired, having cycled, it was calculated, 206,000 miles to work over 23 years from Kington to Leominster. He had 47 years service to his credit, having joined the GWR at Kington in 1915 as a porter. He became a passenger guard on the Leominster and Kington line in 1937 and was stationed at Leominster from 1939, cycling there and back daily.[26]

The railways understandably resented the fact that road transport escaped many of the legal obligations they had to accept by statute. In 1925 there was a correspondence on this subject in the *Kington Times* in which the Leominster secretary of the National Union of Railwaymen argued that the railways were sustaining one-third of the total cost of road construction and maintenance by direct taxation, exclusive of local highway rates. The railways, he said, contributed £7,826,583 to the roads in 1924, so that 19% of their total income went in rates, to the benefit of their commercial opposition.[27]

The Railway Companies' Association pursued a similar theme in December 1938 when a war in Europe was becoming daily more than a possibility, and to gain local support for its national campaign for the right for the railways to fix their own rates and fares took out a full size advertisement in the *Kington Times*, headed 'The Railways ask for a square deal' and making to its readers nine points:

1. In fixing rates for carrying merchandise railways are controlled by statutory regulations passed over the last hundred years and progressively more rigid.
2. No other form of goods transport is subject to such restrictions.
3. No other form of transport has or can have such basic responsibilities to the State, especially at times of National emergency.

4. The railways will not be able to discharge those responsibilities in a time of National emergency unless they are set free to put their house in order and to run their business on business lines.
5. The railways have no desire to interfere with other transport systems and services.
6. They want an opportunity to put themselves right to meet fair competition in a fair way.
7. The time-honoured shackles on railway goods traffic must go and soon to make competition equal.
8. They must go before it is too late.
9. A short Act of Parliament is all that is needed.'

We have seen already how in 1912 it took 4¾ hours to travel to Kington from Birmingham by rail and that the GWR considered the town council had little ground for complaint. In March 1922 there was a petition from the townspeople of Kington for the reinstatement of the late train to Kington which left Leominster at the not very late hour of 8.50 pm. The town council was assured the matter would receive further thought, but the recent restoration of the 7.40 pm Kington-Leominster train had not been a success. On the first day the train had carried but one passenger; on the second day two passengers, and on the third day one passenger.[28]

It was not only at Kington that the rumblings of dissatisfaction were heard. In March 1934 Leominster town council had very heated debate about the railway's failure to put in a competitive tender for the delivery of road chippings needed for the local road improvements which the council had in progress.[29] On the other hand one might well ask by what other way in 1922 could the 300 Australian Orpington pullets which arrived at Kingsland station by passenger train from London, and whose 'condition on arrival gave every indication of robust health,' have made the journey? Likewise in January 1923, when the local press was headlining a double murder sensation, George Buckeridge, who was charged with murdering Mrs Eliza Sainsbury and Mrs Winifred Buckeridge and being in custody, was brought to the inquest at Pembridge by train. The *Kington Times* carried a photograph of him arriving at Pembridge station for the adjourned inquest with two prison warders and his solicitor.[30] How else could he have been brought to and from prison in a day for the local inquest?

The complaints continued to the end. The accommodation at Leominster station for passengers waiting for their connections and the inconvenience of the timing of these connections were a recurring themes throughout the history of the Kington railways, so it is no surprise that in

January 1955, a month before the closure of railway, the Kington Chamber of Trade should have complained there was little provision for outward journeys from Kington of any distance and none for an evening return, and there were always long waits at Leominster, as when one arrived there from Kington at 11.45 am and a man had to wait until 1 pm for the connection to Hereford. The problem received national publicity when in the BBC' s radio programme Town Forum, a panel member described his experiences trying to reach Kington by rail from the Midlands: 'I got to Wolverhampton all right, but it took four and a half hours from Shrewsbury to here, including a two hour wait at Leominster, with no fire or light in the waiting-room.'

The local paper regularly carried detailed reports of forthcoming developments on the GWR in service and stock. But how relevant, for example, to the railway users of Kington and the surrounding area was the news in April 1933 that the GWR was now to run a daily air service between Cardiff, Torquay and Teignmouth? It was of no more than academic interest to the sheep farmers of the Welsh border that this was the first time any British railway company has exercised the powers obtained from Parliament in 1929 to run air services. Or that the journey would take approximately 45 minutes against the four hours previously required, the fare being £3 single; £5 return and that passengers' heavy luggage would go by rail and be delivered, at no extra charge. 'Imperial Airways are providing a three-engined Westland Wessex six-seater plane with one of their most experienced pilots and all the necessary ground staff. The plane will be painted in GWR colours, chocolate and cream, and the interior upholstery will be similar to that used in a first class compartment.'[31]

Later in the same year, in December, the *Kington Times* in its account of GWR Developments, Progress, and Enterprise in 1933 informed its readership of the million pound scheme whereby twenty-ton wagons could be hired by colliery companies and that there were to be faster freight trains for the Midlands and the West of England. They were reminded of what they already knew, namely that Britain's first railway air service now linked Birmingham, Cardiff and Plymouth, though the information that carriage notices for light articles and third class on carriage doors were to be withdrawn was probably more relevant, and the information that penny a mile tickets could be obtained anywhere, any day, any train was, no doubt, reassuring. Day excursion tickets were available from Kington for the Cheltenham races so it may have interested the readers of the *Kington Times* that the thousandth run of the *Cheltenham Flyer*, the world's fastest steam train, had occurred on March 3rd last. The news that Plymouth could now be reached from Paddington in under four hours for the first time was probably of little interest, though the local farming community may have wondered when Kington would see the GWR's new 'double decker cattle trains' or whether it would be worth its while to use the Company's facilities for 'moving farms hundreds of miles between milking times.' The GWR's two million pound programme, it was announced, for 1934 included the introduction of 'Britain's first stream-lined rail car' but again, though such a vehicle could have transformed Kington's facility for locomotion, it was never used locally.[32] Even at a more modest and more practical level, when the GWR introduced camping coach holidays in 1934, despite the indisputably scenic nature of the neighbourhood, the nearest coach was to be at Rhaeadr. The same year, 1934, when the sale of joint rail and road tickets was established at 300 points on the GWR, and once again faithfully reported by the *Kington Times*, nowhere around Kington was involved. The GWR was anxious that the local community should know what was happening elsewhere on its system, but equally indifferent to the possibility of the Kington railways having any part in these developments.

The Kington railways enjoyed a career which was at least remarkably free from accidents. The only major mishap was the crash in 1914 at Kington station mentioned in a previous chapter. Most of the accidents involved railway employees and unpleasant mutilations which the local press reported in objective detail, as when 'A goods yard foreman, Richard Evans, of Knill Street, Leominster, was shunting the cattle train for Hereford market. After signalling to the man in the box to turn the points, turning out the railway lamp and swinging his hand-lamp as a signal to the driver, he went across the rails and his right foot became wedged between the stock rails and he was knocked down by the buffer of the guard's van before he could free himself.'[33] Happily, fatalities were rare, but in October 1922 one involved a Kington boy who was stationed at Kington before going to Hereford as a guard. He was knocked down and decapitated in the goods sidings at Leominster during a shunting operation.[34]

There was another fatality involving a local man in 1933 when in the sidings at Eardisley station a fifty-year-old engine-driver, Mr Alfred James Morgan, of Park View, Kington, and who had been stationed in Kington several years, fell and struck a rail whilst oiling his engine. His fireman was with him, Alfred Leonard Prees, another Kington man, of Hatton Gardens.[35] In 1940 a train hit one of the crossing-gates at the Dolyhir Middle Crossing, which in turn struck the crossing keeper, and her subsequent decline in health and death were ascribed to this mishap. She was the wife of Ganger Powell, the couple having a joint appointment. The saddest fatality was in March 1952 when a two-year-old child, playing on the track, was killed by the 12.30 pm Presteign-Kington goods train at Stansbatch near Staunton on Arrow. It seems that the Kington stationmaster was travelling on the train and it was decided the best course was to take the child by train to the Cottage Hospital at Kington, but the injured child 'died in the stationmaster, Mr Seymour's, arms.'[36]

When mishaps of one kind or another there was a conspicuous readiness on the part of the local railway not only to restore the interrupted service as quickly as possible, but also to minimise its effect upon its few clients. In November 1938 it was reported in the *Kington Times* that 'the Kington line was blocked two and a half miles from Leominster by the fall of a large tree in a gale so that the 9.25 am could not run. A gang of men sent out by motor lorry had it cleared by 11.20. A special train then ran from Kington to connect with Leominster trains.' There was a pride in keeping the railway going whatever the weather so that it was ruled that 'the Engineering Department will attend to the frost fire as necessary at the water column at Kington subject to the over-riding principle that enginemen taking water will be responsible for seeing that when they leave the watering point a good fire is left burning.'[37] When there was snow over the week-end 'the Kington Station Master must arrange to run a light engine over the Branch between Kington and New Radnor and Leominster on the Monday morning, before the first booked train, should such an arrangement be necessary to keep the traffic moving. If it is decided to run an engine early on Monday morning, the Station Masters must advise the Crossing Keepers and Signalmen so that the line may be opened earlier to pass the light engine.'[38] Such was the fall of snow in the winter of 1947 that two 4-4-0 Bulldogs had to come from Worcester to clear the snow-blocked line between Dolyhir and New Radnor.

But on the whole little went wrong on the Kington line which could not be put right locally; things were different on the main line as when in January 1961 the local paper described in great detail how a freight train taking steel from Motherwell to Port Talbot had to stop at Leominster when one of its 40-ton bogie bolster trucks developed a hot axle-box. The truck was removed to a siding and a 30-ton capacity steam crane brought down from Shrewsbury to transfer its cargo of 2 fifteen-ton blocks of steel to another truck.

Railway appointments were news and even the lowliest positions had status in the eyes of the local community.[39] The *Kington Times* regularly reported the promotions, retirements and deaths of local railway men, most of whom served the Company for long periods of service, and it gave summaries of their careers. In May 1913, for example, an account was carried of the presentation made at Kington station by Mr J S Allen, the stationmaster, to Driver William Stanley on his retirement. He was given a silver-mounted umbrella, suitably inscribed, and a pipe and tobacco pouch. This was the public recognition of Driver Stanley's 32 years as an engine-driver on the Leominster and Kington line. He joined the GWR in 1863 and had been with the company for a total of 49 years.[40]

Mr Stanley's record was closely rivalled by that of Mr Parry, who in September 1922 retired after 47 years with the Midland Railway. He was appointed to Eardisley as stationmaster in March 1880, having come from the Swansea Valley where he was appointed stationmaster of Cray in 1879. Amongst his retirement recollections was that of the GWR Eardisley-Titley track being removed 'lock, stock and barrel' in 1916 for France.[41] Like many railwaymen he was active in public life and a keen churchman, serving Eardisley as a school manager and as a member of the parochial church council .

Foreman J Williams of Leominster station could also claim a total of 47 years service at Leominster under six stationmasters and 34 years without missing a day's work. He was now retiring, having joined the service in 1887 as a goods porter, he then moved to the platform as a porter, before returning to the goods department as a relief shunter. Back to the passenger department, working early and late turns as foreman. In 1918 when the eight hour day came into operation he became passenger foreman.[42]

When Mr A J Rawlings, stationmaster of Stanner for eight years, was promoted to be stationmaster of Ballingham near Hereford, his well-attended farewell party was held at Old Radnor Rectory and his service as a chorister, Sunday school teacher, and member of the parochial church council was gratefully acknowledged. A meeting of well wishes was held at Old Radnor rectory.[43]

Some railwaymen even became clergymen whilst others simply bred them. Two years after Mr Rawlings left Stanner in 1929, there was a presentation to Mr F C Brinkwash, a Kington booking-clerk, who was leaving to be trained for the Church. His farewell ceremony took place in the waiting-room at Leominster station at a meeting of the Leominster and District Railwaymen's Club. He had joined the GWR in 1925 at Kemble as a junior clerk and after a year at Kington was now going to Kelham Theological College to train for the priesthood.[44]

On the other hand, when Mr Aaron Griffiths retired in 1930 as stationmaster of Pembridge after forty years service contented himself with having a son who became a clergyman, the vicar of Craven Arms, whilst he himself was a chorister in the parish church, a member of the parochial church council, and chairman of Pembridge football club. He was born in Kington in 1868, the son of Evan Griffiths, a horse trainer and jockey, and joined the GWR in London. In succession he had served as a porter and then a signal-man at Abergavenny, before becoming relief stationmaster at Dolyhir in 1904. He was stationmaster at Peplow for six years, before returning to Dolyhir and New Radnor as stationmaster. He then had spells at Brymbo and Gresford, before returning once again, this time for health reasons, to Dolyhir and Pembridge, and retired to Jessamine Cottage at Floodgates in his home town of Kington where he died in 1941. He was as active in retirement as he was in his working life, singing in the choir of the parish church, taking services in the Kington Mission Room, and acting as secretary to the Kington branch of the League of Nations Union.[45]

Some of these long service biographies narrated the *cursus honorum* available to the committed railwayman. Thus in July 1934 the *Kington Times* reported that 'After forty-six years service on the GWR, Inspector Ernest J Edwards has retired from the post of station inspector at Shrub Hill. Born in Leominster in 1873, he started his railway career as a lad porter at Kington in 1888 and afterwards occupied posts at Leominster, Kington, Hereford, and Ledbury. He was appointed inspector at Evesham in 1912.'

Promotion of course often meant moving and the geographical mobility of local railwaymen as well as their social mobility was faithfully recorded week by week in the *Kington Times*. In September 1911 J C W Reynolds, a clerk from Stonehouse, was appointed clerk at Kington, and in February 1913 Mr Charles Steel, stationmaster at Ruspidge on the diminutive branch from Newnham to Drybrook in the Forest of Dean, was promoted to become stationmaster of New Radnor.[46] Finally, virtue was obviously its own reward in the case of Mr A Williams, the stationmaster of Dolyhir, who in December 1914 after 'eight years of uniform courtesy and efficient work which enabled him to make many friends' secured promotion to become stationmaster of the considerably more important main line station of Gresford near Wrexham.[47]

Other railwaymen were neither promoted, nor did they move, and such a man was Mr Bert Cole of Kington who retired as a plate-layer in July 1929 after 30 years service. He joined the GWR in 1890 at Pembridge and then moved to Kington where he remained for the rest of his working life. At his presentation the chairman listed the services provided for the railway company by its permanent way men: 'Relaying hedges, cutting hedges, grubbing up hedges, sharpening points, swollen by the heat; releasing points, frozen by the frost; setting fire to the hay they had cut beside the line; putting out the fires when the engineman had set fire to the line. They were a helping hand to everyone.'[48]

The work of the platform staff of a country station was not strenuous and there was time enough for the cultivation of station gardens. Indeed Lady Milbank of Norton Manor, daughter of Sir Richard Green Price, bt, maintained the family's railway connection by the 'practice of having the station gardens of, Leominster, Presteign, Eardisley, and New Radnor branches inspected. She awarded prizes for the best of them. In 1907 Dolyhir gained the first prize of thirty shillings, 'a cheque for the amount being accompanied by an encouraging letter from Lady Milbank to the Station Master.'[49] The successful stationmaster was Mr Parry who in 1912, having moved from Dolyhir to Adderley on the Wellington-Crewe line, once again won a GWR station garden competition. According to the *Kington Times* 'Mr Parry's magnificent floral displays in three terraces of flowers and hanging baskets won him the £5 prize for the best kept station in the Chester division of the GWR.'[50]

In November 1932 the *Kington Times* carried an article by the local secretary of the National Union of Railwaymen in response to the railways wanting a further reduction in wages, resulting in an overall reduction of 10%. Despite the economic pressures of the times, the union was resisting this deterioration in its members' wages, arguing that between March 1921 and March 1932 there had been an overall decrease of 200,000 in the number of railway employees, though the net income of the railway companies in 1931 was £33m. Staff reductions and reduced gradings had brought about savings to compensate for falling traffic receipts. In 1932 a locomotive driver received from 12/- to 15/- a day; a fireman 9/- to 11/- a day, 12/- after ten years firing; a plate layer in a rural area earned 6/8d a day; and a signal-man received from 48/- to 75/- a week, according to the classification of his signal-box. Consequently younger railwaymen were looking for more profitable employment elsewhere and the tradition of long service was beginning to falter. At a railway presentation at Leominster the chairman of the proceedings noted that Mr Jones, after eighteen years service and despite the improved conditions of the railway, had found a post in a town the size of Leominster where he could better himself. This, the chairman said, was something of a rebuke to the public which had said nasty things about railwaymen and their rates of pay.[51]

The situation became worse after the war; other jobs seemed more attractive and national service was disruptive. Speaking at a presentation, held this time in what was, no doubt, the rather more congenial atmosphere of Kington's Railway Tavern, as opposed to the station waiting-room, to Mr H Brooks, on his retirement after 42 years service, Mr Frank Seymour, the stationmaster, made the point in his speech that younger men were not adequate replacements, for they did not stay long enough to learn the job adequately. As soon as a better-paid job appeared elsewhere they went for it and national service did not help either, for having spent two years learning the ways of the railway, they were then called up. Until the railway service was made more attractive than other industries, Mr Seymour was convinced, young men would not make it their career.[52]

The railway offered its servants their own distinctive form of social life and in February 1923, for example, railwaymen from Kington, Titley, and Presteign stations were entertained at the Burton Hotel, Kington. Their numbers are significant: 10 came from Kington; 4 from Presteign; and 3 from Titley. Songs were sung after dinner and a toast drunk to 'The Railways'. In his speech, the Kington stationmaster, Mr J E Perkin, justified the recently introduced higher fares and freight rates. Safety, said he, had to be paid for. Nevertheless 'an enjoyable evening ended with the singing of the National Anthem.'[53]

Another popular feature of the local railwayman's social life was the GWR Sectional Ambulance competition for the Horlick Shield. In 1933 the Kington team was pleased to be placed 8th in the competition held that year at Gloucester. In 1939, according to the *Kington Times*, ' The Kington team did extremely well in the Ambulance Competition.' One of the tasks was to deal with a jockey's fall in a hurdle race and here 'the Kington team excelled in carrying out the considerable amount of first aid attention necessary to the jockey and finally conveying the injured man to hospital.' Another world war, however, was at the threshold when rather more serious demands of first aid would be needed than dealing with injured steeple-chasing jockeys.

In the line's last years the trains between Leominster and New Radnor were manned by Leominster based staff, but two permanent way gangs were stationed at Kington, one for track maintenance between Kington and Kington Junction, Leominster, where the line left the main line, and the other for maintaining the track between Kington and New Radnor. One of the gangers responsible for the maintenance of this track was Mr G Abberley, of the engineering department of Kingsland, where he started work in 1897 and in the course of 41 years worked under 13 different inspectors. In 1934 he won first prize for the best kept length of line in the area.[54]

In January 1946 a relief fireman worked on a Leominster-New Radnor train and has left an account of his experiences running over Ganger Abberley's section of line. It is somewhat romanticised, for he saw eagles from his footplate which others would identify more certainly as buzzards and hills become in his eyes mountains. The 'little stream' is the River Arrow which when in flood could bring the railway, which followed its course more or less all the way from New Radnor to Leominster, to a complete halt. This was the case, for example, in December 1929 when the *Kington Times* reported 'Worst floods at Kington in living memory. The permanent way at the railway station was flooded to the depth of nearly a foot and the afternoon and evening services to and from New Radnor were cancelled.'[55]

All the same, the account has something of the atmosphere of this border line in its last days and his description of the procedures followed on it are, no doubt, accurate. It is an appropriate ending for this account of the history of a small border town and the railways which served it for just over a century:

'At Kington we again took on water. From here we were in a land of our own, one train only working. That meant until we returned no other train could enter the single line. The line left Kington with the small loco shed on the right, it was about large enough to house two small tanks. Passing here the line rose steeply through very tight twists and turns through trees and skirting a little stream with kingfishers darting about until it made its way out into the open to a little halt called Stanner. From here eagles could be seen swirling and soaring among the crags of the rocky hills. On tp the next little stop at Dolyhir. From a position nearing here three distant signals came into view all at the same time, odd for this type of line, they were only for level-crossing gates. Further on the line weaved through mountains climbing all the way until it came to its end at the foot of a mountain.

At the terminus we were booked five minutes in which time I had to uncouple and run the loco forward over the points. Then I walked to the ground frame, unlocked it, turned the points and, after the driver had run into the loop, then had to close the points, get back on board to go to the other end and open the points for the driver to come over and return the train. After locking the points I had the pleasure of recoupling the loco. With a fast driver one day we tried to see how long or at least how quickly we could do it. The shortest time was nine minutes, a guaranteed five minutes late start back. The run back was very interesting, the driver opened the regulator and after a few puffs shut off to freewheel for what seemed miles. Leaving Radnor the view was spectacular, mountains everywhere, valleys filled with trees. I gazed on several occasions trying to find which way we would eventually go but never did sort it out, we were soon in the trees with no hope of seeing anything.'[56]

NOTES

1. KT 5.3.1910.
2. KT 28.10.1932.
3. Ibid.
4. KT 24.12.1932.
5. KT 18.2.1933.
6. KT 19.8.1933.
7. KT 24.8.1935.
8. KT 4.11.1950.
9. KT 29.7.1954.
10. KT 19.10.1919.
11. Dunabin, op.cit.,p.19
12. Ibid.,p.13.
13. Ibid.,p.36.
14. Ibid.,p.37.
15. Ibid.,p.44.
16. Ibid.,p.92.
17. Ibid.
18. KT 12. 8. 1933.
19. Ibid.
20. KT 2.10.1937.
21. KT 3.12.1938.
22. KT 15. 2.1951.
23. KT 20.4.1935.
24. KT 30.12.1933.
25. Thus the KT 8:5:1909 announced the death of Alice Drew after a long illness, 'She was the wife of Arthur Drew, a drayman employed by the GWR at Kington station.'
26. KT 1.2.1962.
27. KT 26.12.1925.
28. KT 15. 4.1922.
29. KT 10. 4.1934.
30. KT 13.1.1923.

31. KT 8.4.1933.
32. KT 30.12.1933.
33. KT 7.12.1912.
34. KT 21.10.1922.
35. KT 13.5.1933.
36. KT 29.3.1952.
37. Appendix to the Western Region 1955 No 12 Service Time Table, p.106
38. GWR Regulations.
39. KT 9.9.1911.
40. KT 2.2.1913.
41. KT 3. 9.1922.
42. KT 16. 6.1938.
43. KT 25. 7.1927.
44. KT 30.10.1929.
45. KT 1.2.1930; 22.3.1941.
46. KT 2.2.1913. In 1922 Ruspidge was described in Bradshaw's *Railway Guide* as a halt and passengers were warned it was served by 'auto-cars one class only,' so coming to New Radnor was indeed a promotion.
47. KT 22.12.1914.
48. KT 20.7.1929.
49. *The Great Western Railway Magazine*, Oct 1907, p.230.
50. KT 10.2.1912.
51. KT 16.4.1927.
52. KT 10.5.1952.
53. KT 3.2.1923.
54. KT 14.1.1939.
55. KT 14.12.1929.
56. Jack Gardner, *Castles to Warships: on the Great Western footplate*, London, 1986, p. 102.

TIME-TABLES
Time-table of the Leominster and Kington Railway, July 1866

	Week days					Sundays	
	Mail	1st 2nd	1st 2nd	1st 2nd	1st 2nd	Goods	1st 2nd
	1st 2nd	*Parliam.	Parliam.	Parliam.	Parliam.	Mail	Parliam.
						1st 2nd	
						Parliam.	
Kington:	7.40	11.00	1.30	3.55	7.45	8.00	7.45
Titley:	7.50	11.05	1.40	4.00	7.50	8.08	7.50
Pembridge:	8.10	11.15	2.00	4.10	8.00	8.20	8.00
Kingsland:	8.20	11.25	2.15	4.20	8.10	8.30	8.10
Leominster:	8.35	11.35	2.30	4.30	8.20	8.45	8.20
Leominster:	5.20	9.45	12.00	2.55	6.35	5.20	6.50
Kingsland:	5.40	10.00	12.15	3.09	6.50	5.40	7.05
Pembridge:	5.50	10.10	12.30	3.18	6.58	5.50	7.13
Titley:	6.05	10.24	12.50	3.35	7.15	6.05	7.30
Kington:	6.10	10.30	1.00	3.40	7.20	6.10	7.35

(*The Regulations of Railways Act 1844 required railway companies to provide covered third class carrages and to run at least one 1d a mile *Parliamentary* train a day).

Connections at Leominster

	Week Days							
Hereford Barr's Court:		8.15	9.05	12.35	2.15		5.05	7.55
Barton:						3.10	4.05	7.50
Moreton:			9.18		2.27		5.17	
Dinmore Station:		8.32			2.34		5.25	8.14
Ford Bridge:			9.32		2.42		5.33	
Leominster:	7.15	8.44	9.38	1.05	2.50	3.35	5.39	8.25
Berrington:	7.23	8.52			2.57		5.49	
Woofferton:	7.30	9.03	9.54		3.05	3.48	5.57	8.36
Ludlow:		9.15	10.06	1.25	3.17	3.58	6.12	8.46
Bromfield:					3.23		6.19	
Onibury:			10.16		3.33		6.29	8.55
Craven Arms:		9.32	10.26	1.40	3.43	4.14	6.39	9.03
Marsh Brook:			10.40		3.53		6.50	
Church Stretton:		9.48	10.50	1.56	4.06	4.30	7.00	9.20

Week Days continued

Leebotwood:				4.15		7.11	
Dorrington:		11.05		4.23		7.19	9.35
Condover:				4.28		7.24	
Shrewsbury:	10.12	11.25	2.25	4.40	4.55	7.35	9.50

Shrewsbury:	3.15	7.00	10.25	12.25	1.40	2.45	5.00	8.15
Condover:		7.12		12.37		2.57		8.30
Dorrington:		7.18		12.42		3.03		8.35
Leebotwood:		7.28		12.52		3.13		8.45
Church Stretton:		7.40		1.02		3.25	5.30	8.57
Marsh Brook:		7.47		1.09		3.32		9.05
Craven Arms:	4.17	7.59	11.02	1.20	2.18	3.44	5.45	9.18
Onibury:		8.08		1.28		3.53		9.25
Bromfield:		8.14		1.34		3.59		9.30
Ludlow:	4.45	8.22	11.17	1.41	2.33	4.07	6.03	9.35
Woofferton:		8.34	11.27	1.51		4.19	6.15	9.45
Berrington:		8.43		1.59		4.27		9.53
Leominster:	5.14	8.52	11.45	2.07	2.53	4.35	6.30	10.00
Ford Bridge:		8.58		2.13		4.41		10.05
Dinmore:		9.08		2.23		4.51	6.43	10.15
Moreton:		9.14		2.32		5.00		10.23
Hereford Barr's Court:		9.30	12.15	2.47		5.20	7.05	10.35
Barton:					3.20			

Sundays

Hereford Barr's Court:		7.55
Barton:	11.30	
Moreton:	11.45	
Dinmore:	11.55	
Ford Bridge:	12.05	
Leominster:	12.10	8.25
Berrington:	12.20	
Woofferton:	12.30	8.36
Ludlow:	12.45	8.46
Bromfield:	12.51	
Onibury:	12.57	8.55
Craven Arms:	1.05	9.03
Marsh Brook:	1.17	
Church Stretton:	1.25	9.20
Leebotwood:	1.33	
Dorrington:	1.40	9.35
Condover:	1.45	
Shrewsbury:	1.55	9.50

Shrewsbury	3.15	4.50
Condover		5.04
Dorrington		5.10
Leebotwood		5.20
Church Stretton		5.30
Marsh Brook		5.38
Craven Arms	4.20	5.50
Onibury		5.58
Bromfield		6.04
Ludlow	4.48	6.10
Woofferton		6.22
Berrington		6.32
Leominster	5.18	6.40
Ford Bridge		6.45
Dinmore		6.53
Moreton		7.00
Hereford Barr's Court		
Barton		7.20

Time-table of the Leominster and Kington Railway, 1922

Kington:	7.20	11.12*	2.57*	6.22*	7.40	
Titley:	7.25	11.17	3.02	6.27	7.45	
Pembridge:	7.35	11.27	3.12	6.37	7.55	
Kingsland:	7.41	11.36	3.21	6.47	8.04	
Leominster:	7.51	11.43	3.28	6.54	8.11	
Leominster:	6.30	9.54	12.45	4.45	6.00	8.54
Kingsland:	6.41	10.03	12.54	4.54	6.09	9.03
Pembridge:	6.51	10.11	1.02	5.02	6.17	9.11
Titley:	7.05	10.22	1.13	5.13	6.27	9.22
Kington:	7.10	10.26+	1.17+	5.17+	6.31	9.26

* Starts at New Radnor
+ Continued to New Radnor

Time-table of the Leominster, Kington, New Radnor,
& Presteign Railways, 1944

Week days only

Leominster, Kington, and New Radnor

Leominster:	6.18	9.50		12.35	4.55	
Kingsland:	6.29	9.59		12.50	5.04	
Pembridge:	6.38	10.07		1.02	5.12	
Marston Halt:	6.44	10.12		1.09	5.17	
Titley:	6.53	10.20	11.19	1.17	5.24	6.17
Kington arr:	6.57	10.24	11.22	1.24	5.28	6.21
dep:		10.28			5.33	
Stanner Halt:		10.35			5.40	
Dolyhir:		10.39			5.44	
New Radnor:		10.45			5.50	
New Radnor:			10.52			6.05
Dolyhir:			10.58			6.11
Stanner Halt:			11.02			6.15
Kington arr:			11.10			6.21
dep:	7.21	10.30	11.14	2.00	5.20	6.27
Titley:	7.26	10.33	11.18	2.03	5.24	6.32
Marston Halt:	7.31		11.23	2.09		6.37

Pembridge:	7.37	11.29	2.16	6.43
Kingsland:	7.46	11.38	2.26	6.52
Leominster:	7.55	11.45	2.33	7.02

Titley and Presteign:

Weekdays only

Kington:	10.30	5.20
Titley:	10.34	5.28
Forge Crossing Halt:	10.37	5.33
Presteign:	10.46	5.44

Presteign:	11.02	6.00
Forge Crossing Halt:	11.11	6.10
Titley:	11.14	6.16
Kington:	11.22	6.21

Kington & Eardisley
Service suspended

Time-table of the Kington and Eardisley Railway, 1875

Kington:		9.20	12.20	6.25
Titley:	7.45	9.25	12.25	6.30
Lyonshall:	7.50	9.30	12.30	6.35
Almeley:	8.00	9.40	12.40	6.45
Eardisley:	8.05	9.45	12.45	6.50

Eardisley:	8.20	10.50	2.35	7.02
Almeley:	8.25	10.55	2.40	7.07
Lyonshall:	8.40	11.10	2.55	7.20
Titley:	8.45	11.15	3.00	7.25
Kington:	8.50	11.20	3.05	7.30

Time-table of the Kington and Eardislay Railway, 1884

Kington:	9.00	11.15	3.25	6.30
Titley:	9.05	11.22	3.32	6.35
Lyonshall:	9.16	11.27	3.39	6.40
Almeley:	9.30	11.37	3.52	6.50
Eardisley:	9.35	11.42	3.57	6.55

Eardisley:		9.53	12.00	4.16	7.05
Almeley:		9.58	12.10	4.21	7.10
Lyonshall:		10.12	12.28	4.35	7.25
Titley:		10.17	12.38	4.40	7.30
Kington:		10.22	12.42	4.45	7.35

Timetable of the New Radnor Railway 1875

Kington:	6.45	10.32	11.32	2.20	5.00
Stanner:	6.54	10.41	11.41	2.29	5.09
Dolyhir:	6.59	10.46	11.46	2.34	5.14
New Radnor:	7.05	10.52	11.52	2.40	5.20
New Radnor:	7.20	10.57	11.57	2.45	6.55
Dolyhir:	7.27	11.03	12.03	2.52	7.02
Stanner:	7.32	11.08	12.08	2.57	7.07
Kington:	7.40	11.15	12.15	3.05	7.15

Time-table of the New Rador Railway, 1884

Kington:	10.30	1.45	5.05
Stanner:	10.39	1.57	5.15
Dolyhir:	10.44	2.03	5.24
New Radnor:	10.50	2.09	5.30
New Radnor:	10.55	2.15	6.00
Dolyhir:	11.01	2.22	6.07
Stanner:	11.06	2.27	6.12
Kington:	11.13	2.35	6.20

Timetable of the New Radnor Railway, 1922

Kington:	10.29*	1.55*	5.30*
Stanner:	10.37	2.03	5.38
Dolyhir:	10.41	2.07.	5.42
New Radnor:	10.47	2.13	5.48
New Radnor:	10.52	2.30	6.00
Dolyhir:	10.58	2.36	6.06
Stanner:	11.02	2.40	6.10
Kington:	11.12+	2.57+	6.22+

* Started at New Radnor
+ Continued to New Radnor

Time-table of the Presteign Railway, 1875

Kington:	6.50	10.15	11.17	3.30	6.55
Titley arrive:	6.54	10.20	11.22	3.34	6.59
depart:	6.55	10.30	11.25	3.35	7.00
Presteign:	7.10	10.45	11.40	3.50	7.15
Presteign:	7.15	11.00	11.45	4.20	7.23
Titley arrive:	7.20	11.15	11.59	4.34	7.37
depart:	7.30	11.22	12.00	4.35	7.40
Kington:	7.35	11.27	12.05	4.40	7.45

Time-table of Presteign Railway, 1922

Kington:	10.30	1.09	5.22	6.42*
Titley arrive:	10.34	1.13	5.26	6.46
depart:	10.36	1.16	5.28	6.48
Presteign:	10.48	1.30	5.40	7.00
Presteign:	10.55	2.43	6.03	7.10*
Titley arrive:	11.09	2.57	6.17	7.24
depart:	11.17	3.02	6.18	7.25
Kington:	11.21	3.06	6.22	7.29

* Wednesdays only
No Sunday Service

Time-table on the restoration of the Eardisley-Titley Junction line, 1922

Weekdays only

	Mixed	Passenger	Mixed
New Radnor:		10.52	2.30
Kington:	9.00	11.17	3.25
Presteign:		10.55	
Leominster:	6.20		2.43
Titley:	6.50	11.09	2.57
Leominster:		9.50	12.45
Titley:		10.18	1.13
Titley:	9.05	11.22	3.30
Lyonshall:	9.10	11.27	3.35
Almeley:	9.25	11.37	3.50
Eardisley Junction:	9.38	11.42	4.00
Eardisley Junction:	9.56	1.20	4.34
Hay:	10.12	1.35	4.50
Brecon:	11.00	2.35	5.38
Eardisley Junction:		11.46	6.58
Hereford:		12.20	7.51

	Passenger	Mixed	Passenger
Hereford:	9.20		12.45
Eardisley Junction:	9.54		1.20
Brecon:	7.00	10.30	1.10
Hay:	7.46	11.25	2.07
Eardisley Junction:	8.00	11.47	2.23
Eardisley Junction:	9.57	12.00	4.40
Almeley:	10.02	12.06	4.45
Lyonshall:	10.13	12.27	4.56
Titley:	10.17	12.42	5.01
Titley:	11.17	3.02	6.27
Leominster:	11.43	3.28	6.57
Titley:	10.31	1.20	5.28
Presteign:	10.43	1.34	5.40
Kington:	10.22	12.50	5.05
New Radnor:	10.43	2.15	5.48

II

The old gas works, Kington, with Tramway wagons in the foreground.

(Kington Museum)

III

(Kington Museum)

The Kington Tramway passing under Castle Hill House, Kington.

IV   Tram body found at Dolyhir 1963.   *(Kington Museum)*

V   Lyonshall Wharf on the Kington Tramway.   *(L Banks)*

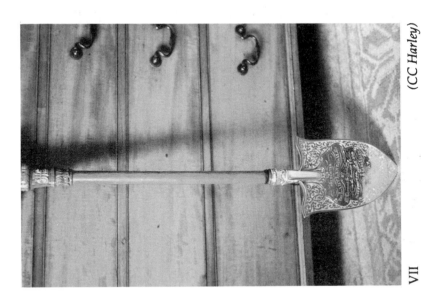

VII   (CC Harley)
Spade used to cut the first sod
of the Kington & Eardisley Railway 1863.

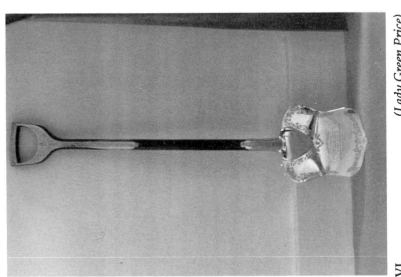

VI   (Lady Green Price)
Spade used to cut
the first sod of the Presteign Railway 1872.

VIII   *(CC Harley)*

Detail of the spade, designed by WL Banks, and used by Lady Langdale in 1863.

IX   (CC Harley)
Silhouette of Lady Langdale.

X   (L Banks)   XI   (L Banks)
Silhouette of James Crummer.   Silhouette of James Davies.

XII   *(Kington Museum)*
Armstrong 517 Class 0-4-2T No 525 arriving at New Radnor Station c.1906.

XIII   *(Kington Museum)*
Gangers and their trolley at New Radnor Station c.1900.

XIV   New Radnor Station 1991, now a touring caravan site.   *(Cadoc Books)*

XV   Goods Shed, New Radnor Station 1991, now a barn.   *(Cadoc Books)*

XVI   Dolyhir Station with its prize winning floral display.   (H Jones)

XVII   Dolyhir: the station and its station master c.1900.   (C Leversedge)

XVIII   One of the Swindon 1701 Class tank   *(R Pritchard)*
engines 0-6-0 poses outside Dolyhir Station c.1895.

XIX   A Volvo BM model L 90 Loading Shovel   *(Cadoc Books)*
rests outside Dolyhir Station, now an electrical workshop, 1991.

XX A Railway family: Ganger Powell, his wife, *(G Layton)*
children, and dog, outside Dolyhir Middle Crossing Keeper's cottage, c.1910.

XXI GWR 57XX Class 0-6-0PT with freight *(EP Jobson)*
train passes Dolyhir Middle Crossing Keeper's cottage, c.1945.

XXII *(Brunel University, Mowat Collection)*
Stanner: general view of station and yard in 1932.

XXIII Stanner Station, 1991: now a store *(Cadoc Books)*
for the Highways Department of Powys County Council.

XXIV   Building the original Kington Station in 1854.   *(Allan Lloyd)*

XXV   *(Allan Lloyd)*
Group photograph of railway staff at Kington Station c.1905.

XXVI   *(EP Jobson)*
The second Kington Station c.1900 with an original Leominster & Kington
GWR coach now being used as a platelayer's shed.

XXVII   GWR lorries at the Goods Shed, Kington Station.   *(G Gregory)*

XXVIII   Flooding at Kington Station.   *(G Gregory)*

XXXIX   Flooding at Kington Station with the Presteign bus in the background.   *(G Gregory)*

XXX   Postcard of the 1914 crash at Kington.   *(G Gregory)*

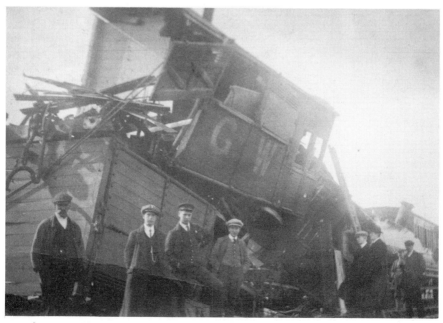

XXXI   Another postcard of the 1914 crash at Kington.   *(G Gregory)*

XXXII   Eardisley Station and its staff c.1900.   *(K Player)*

XXXIII   GWR locomotive shunts at the Midland Eardisley   *(K Player)*
Station after the line to Hay on Wye was abandoned.

XXXIV   Eardisley Station and its staff with a *(K Player)*
Midland train c.1900, bound for Hereford.

XXXV   Eardisley Station in 1991. *(Cadoc Books)*

XXXVI   *(Brunel University, Mowat Collection)*
Eardisley Junction signal box in 1932:
the line from Titley joins the Hereford line from the left.

XXXVII   The same scene in 1991.   *(Cadoc Books)*

XXXVIII   *(Brunel University, Mowat Collection)*
Almeley Station in 1932 with goods yard in the background.

XXXIX   Almeley Station in 1991.   *(Cadoc Books)*

XL   Lyonshall Station in 1932.   *(Brunel University, Mowat Collection)*

XLI   Lyonshall Station, now a dwelling house, in 1991.   *(Cadoc Books)*

XLII   *(EP Jobson)*
Titley Junction c.1905. A passenger train approaches from Eardisley.

XLIII   The same scene in 1932.   *(Brunel University, Mowat Collection)*

XLIV   Titley Junction Station in 1932.   *(Brunel University, Mowat Collection)*

XLV   The six wheeled water tank   *(Cadoc Books)*
which served Titley Station, now in preservation.

XLVI   Presteign Station c.1880.   *(C Leversedge)*
An excursion to the Crystal Palace is advertised in the station notice board.

XLVII   Presteign Station c.1880.   *(C Leversedge)*
The station staff and the town's police sergeant pose for the photographer.

XLVIII   (C Leversedge)
Presteign Station c.1910. A Swindon 1701 Class 0-6-0ST heads a train of two
coaches and a guard's van, all four wheelers, arriving from Kington.

XLIX   Presteign Station c.1914, waiting for the Kington train.   (EP Jobson)

L   (C Leversedge)
Presteign Station c.1919. Four wheeler carriages are still in use.

LI   (C Leversedge)
British Railways inspection saloon at Presteign before the closure of the line
to goods traffic in 1964. Note that the nationalized railways have altered the
correct Welsh spelling of Presteign to the anglicized Presteigne.

LII   Presteign Station. A 517 Class 0-4-2T   *(C Leversedge)*
heading a Kington passenger train is admired by a group of local schoolboys.

LIII   Knighton-Presteign bus.   *(C Leversedge)*
Its driver is the fifth boy from the right in the photograph above.

LIV   *(Cadoc Books)*
The Forge Crossing Bridge over the Arrow, looking downstream.

LV   *(Cadoc Books)*
The Forge Crossing Bridge showing the massive embankment it carried.

LVI   Pembridge Station, 1932.   *(Brunel University, Mowat Collection)*

LVII   *(Cadoc Books)*

The Goods Shed, Pembridge, showing its arcaded brickwork.

LVIII   Kingsland Station, 1932.   *(Brunel University, Mowat Collection)*

LVIX   Kingsland Station, 1991, now a pair of private houses.   *(Cadoc Books)*

LX   *(Brunel University, Mowat Collection)*
Leominster Station, 1930,
with its distinctive central elevated signal box and water tower.

LXI   *(Cadoc Books)*
Leominster Station, 1991 much reduced in size and deserted.

LXII   517 Class 0-4-2T, built at Swindon 1904.   *(C Llewellin)*

LXIII   *(EP Jobson)*
58XX Class 0-4-2T 5807 waiting at New Radnor with the train for Kington.

LXIV   14XX Class 0-4-2T 1420 at   *(G Gregory)*
Kington in 1964 with the last freight train for Presteign.

LXV   *(G Gregory)*
Mr Ernest Gregory, last stationmaster of Kington, 1960-64.

LXVI   Shunting at Kington in   *(G Gregory)*
the final days with a open verandahed GWR 20T brake van.

LXVII   Again, the last days of 1420 at Kington.   *(G Gregory)*

LXVIII   0-4-2T near New Radnor.   *(EP Jobson)*

LXIX   0-6-0PT with a pick-up freight near Dolyhir cottages.   *(EP Jobson)*

LXX   *(Allan Lloyd)*
Pre-World War II Thorneycroft GWR lorry stationed at Kington.

LXXI   Its 1964 equivalent at Kington.   *(G Gregory)*

LXXII   Local emigrants for Canada at   *(C Leversedge)*
Leominster Station: the railways facilitated depopulation.

LXXIII   Leaving Presteign by train for the first World War.   *(C Leversedge)*

LXXIV   *(Cadoc Books)*

Keeper's Cottage, Cobnash Crossing, near Kingsland, 1991, now a private
house: the bed of the track can be seen on the left hand side of the cottage.

LXXV   *(Cadoc Books)*

Keeper's Cottage, Dolyhir East Crossing, now a private house.

LXXVI   0-4-2T 1420 hauling the last   *(Allan Lloyd)*
freight train to Presteign at Bullock's Mill near Kington.

LXXVII   Old Radnor Lime Roadstone & General   *(H Jones)*
Company wagons, with wooden buffers at Kington at the
end of the 19th century. Thatch is still used for roofing local buildings.

LXXVIII   *(B. Lawrence)*

Share certificate of the Leominster and Kington Railway 1854.

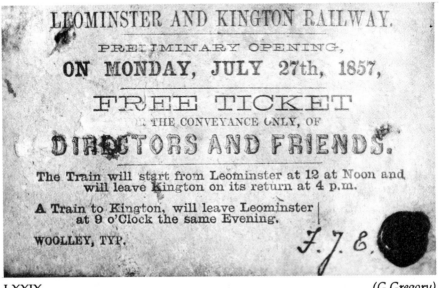

LXXIX   *(G Gregory)*

Ticket for the opening of the Leominster and Kington Railway 1857.

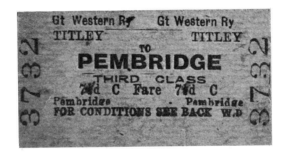

LXXX   Selection of tickets for February 5th 1955,   (H Pinches)
the day the final passenger service from Kington:
Note the use of 'GWR' despite 8 years of nationalization.

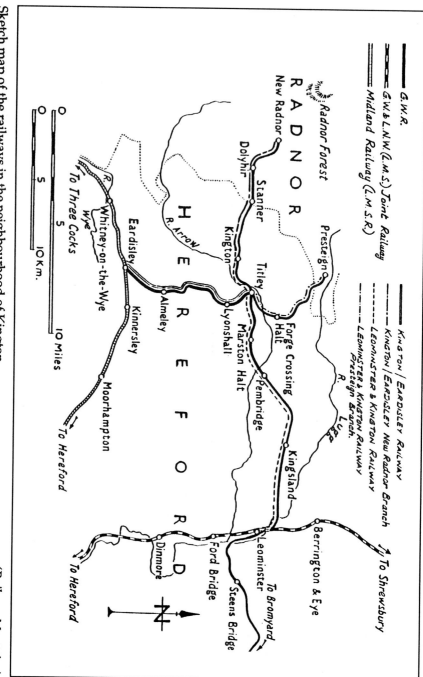

Sketch map of the railways in the neighbourhood of Kington.

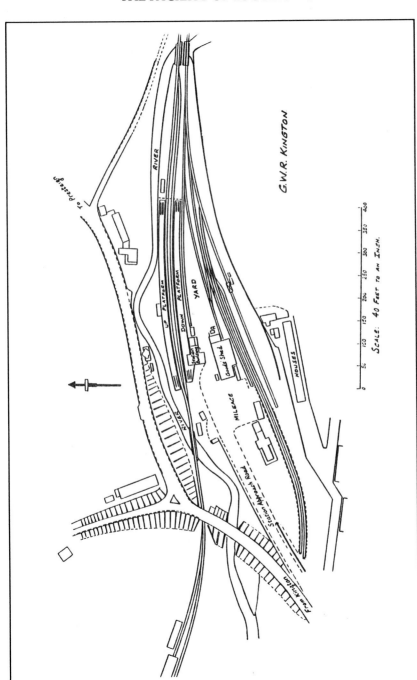

Track diagram of Kington Station c.1935.

(*Railway Magazine*)

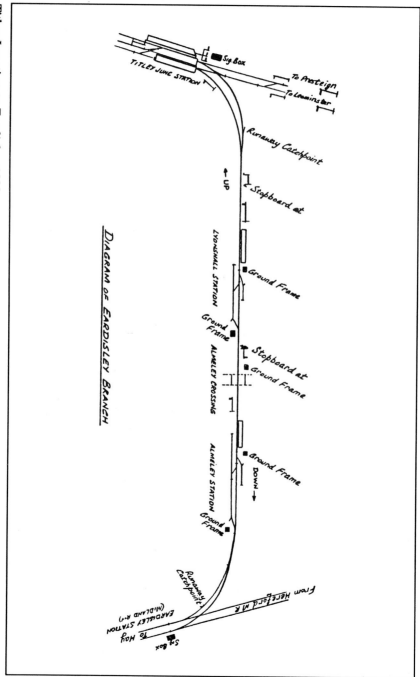

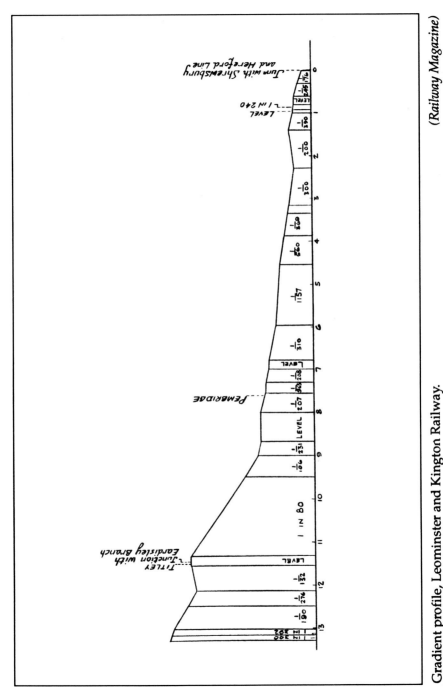

(*Railway Magazine*)

Gradient profile, Leominster and Kington Railway.

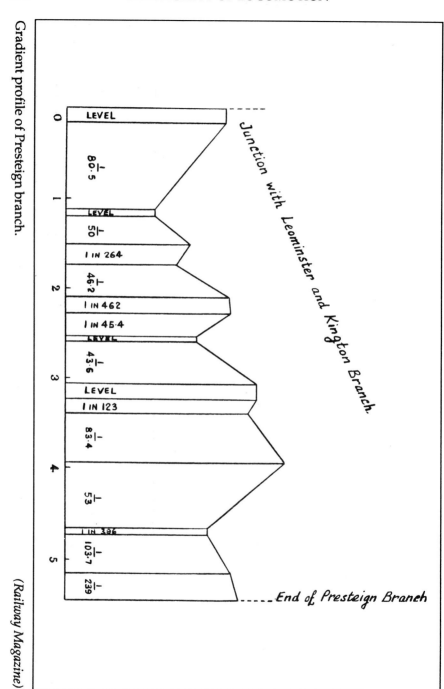

Gradient profile of Presteign branch.

(*Railway Magazine*)

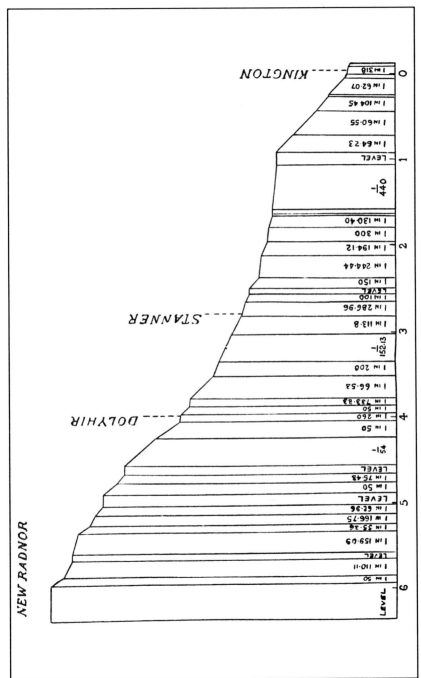

(Railway Magazine)

Gradient profile from Kington to New Radnor.

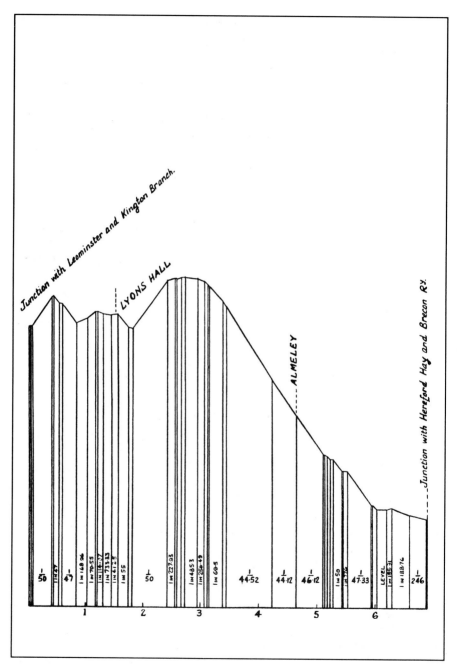

Gradient profile, Eardisley branch.

(Railway Magazine)

Bibliography

ABC Railway Guide, London, 1859.

Alderman, G, *The Railway Interest,* Leicester, 1973.

Baughan, PE, *North and Mid Wales,* Vol 11, A Regional History of the Railways of Great Britain, Newton Abbot, 1980.

Beck, KM, *The West Midland Lines of the GWR,* London, 1983.

Bidde, G, and Nock, OS, *The Railway Heritage of Britain,* London, 1983.

Booth, J, *The Day War Broke Out,* Westbury, 1984.

Bradshaw's Directors' Directory, 1869, Newton Abbot, 1969.

Bradshaw's July 1922 Railway Guide, London, 1985.

Cambrian Traveller's Guide, London, 1813.

Clinker, CR, *The Hay Railway,* Dawlish, 1960.

Clinker, CR, 'The Railways of West Herefordshire', *Transactions of the Woolhope Naturalists' Field Club, XXXV, 1957.*

Cohen, I, 'The Leominster-Stourport Canal', *Transactions of the Woolhope Naturalists' Field Club, XXXV, 1957.*

Coleman, VH, 'The Kington Railway', *Transactions of the Woolhope Naturalists' Field Club,* XXXVIII, 1964.

Cook, RA and Clinker, CR, *Early Railways between Abergavenny and Hereford,* Oakham, 1984.

Dunabin, JE, *The Hereford Bus,* St Albans, 1986.

Ellison, FB, 'The History of the Hay Railway, 1810-1864', *Transactions of the Woolhope Naturalists' Field Club, 1935*

Fenn, RWD, and Roberts, NT, 'The Recollections of Laura Meredith', *Transactions of the Radnorshire Society, LX, 1989.*

Fenn, RWD, and Sinclair, JB, 'Our Ubiquitous Friend', SW Williams, 1837-1899', *Transactions of the Radnorshire Society,* LIX, 1989.

Fenn, RWD, 'Sir Richard Green Price of Norton Manor, 1803-1887', *Transactions of the Radnorshire Society,* LV, 1985.

Haines, A, *Leominster's Twentieth Century Characters and its Poacher,* Leominster, 1988.

Hewitt, JD, 'The Kington Branch of the GWR', *Railway Magazine,* September, 1939.

Higginbotham, J, *Kington Camp,* Kington, 1980.

Holden, JS, *The Manchester-Milford Railway,* Tarrant Hinton 1979.

Howse, WH, *Kington, Herefordshire, Memorials of an old Town,* Kington, 1989.

Howse, WH, *Radnorshire,* Hereford, 1949.

Howse, WH, *Radnor Old and New,* Kington, 1989.

Husband, JF, 'Some Border Bye-ways of the Great Western Railway', *Railway Magazine,* March, 1910.

Jenkins, RT, ed, *The Dictionary of Welsh Biography down to 1940*, London, 1959.

Jobson, EP, *Pansies and Periwinkles*, New Radnor, 1990.

Kidner, RW, *The Mid-Wales Railway*, Oxford, 1990.

Mowat, CL, *The Golden Valley Railway*, Cardiff, 1964.

Oldham, J, ed, *The Diaries of Thomas Carleton Skarratt, Draper of Kington Herefordshire*, Kington, 1987.

Parry, R, *History of Kington*, Kington, 1845.

Partridge, EJ, *The Route of the Shrewsbury and Hereford Railway*, Leominster, 1860.

Oppitz, L, *Hereford and Worcester Railways Remembered*, Newbury, 1990.

Robinson, CJ, *A History of the Mansions and Manors of Herefordshire*, London and Hereford, 1872.

Simmons, J, *The Railway in Town and Country 1830-1914*, Newton Abbot, 1986.

Simmons, J, *The Railways of Britain*, 3rd ed., London, 1986.

Southwood, J, ed, *The Further Recordings of Richard Parry the Kington Historian*, Kington, 1984.

Southwood, J, *The Meredith Family of Presteigne and Kington 1391-1940*, Kington, 1988.

Taylor, AJP, *English History 1914-1945*, Oxford, 1965.

Williams, J, *A General History of the County of Radnorshire*, Brecon, 1905.

Williams, WR, *Herefordshire Members 1213-1896*, Brecon, 1896.

*   *   *   *   *   *

Archaeologia Cambrensis, the Journal of the Cambrian Archaeological Association.

Banks Archives, Kington, Herefordshire.

Bradshaw's Directors' and Shareholders' Directories.

Crockford's Clerical Directories.

The Great Western Railway Magazine.

The Hereford Journal.

The Hereford Times.

The Kington Times.

The Transactions of the Radnorshire Society.

The Transactions of the Woolhope Naturalists' Field Club.

The Railway Magazine.

The Herefordshire County Record Office, Hereford.

The Public Record Office, Kew, Surrey.

INDEX

For ease of identification the pre-1974 county names have been used.